MW01118683

# Quiet Moments

## and

# Holy Places:

# Reflections in Solitude

# Quiet Moments

## and

# Holy Places:

## Reflections in Solitude

by James A. Belcher

FORWARD MOVEMENT PUBLICATIONS
Cincinnati, Ohio

**Forward Movement Publications**

412 Sycamore Street, Cincinnati, Ohio 45202
www.forwardmovement.org
800-543-1813

*For*
*Ella, David*
*and Matthew*

# Contents

# Contents

# Foreword

I am a Christian, a sinner forgiven and saved by grace. I invited Jesus Christ into my life at a church camp on a muggy June night in 1971. I was twenty years old and had no idea what the future had in store for me. But I dared to believe that Jesus could forgive my mistakes, heal my wounds, and create order from the chaos that characterized my adolescent existence.

Since that evening three decades ago, my life has taken many twists and turns, all, I trust, under the watchful care of the heavenly Father. In the last ten years God offered me an unexpected blessing— the blessing of solitude. As I entered my forties, I increasingly felt a need to examine the standards of the cultural, familial, religious, and vocational milieus which framed my existence. In the process I became aware of a chasm between society's value system and my ideals. I recognized that, much of the time, social mores and the expectations of others exerted more influence over my life than my personal code of conduct did.

As I moved in the direction of a more solitary, spiritual lifestyle, activities and concerns which once consumed large portions of my time and energy became less important. I found myself attracted to new, exciting activities. I became drawn to forest trails, deserted beaches, remote mountaintops and quaint coffeehouses—places that had not captured my fascination before the desire for solitude took root in my soul. I experienced a renewed interest in praying and reading, and I began setting aside longer periods of time for silent meditation and for delving into ancient and modern writers in the field of spiritual formation. These periods of solitary reflection became times of renewal from the stress created by vocational demands. They proved to be the fertile soil my soul needed in which to cultivate a deeper relationship with God.

My prayer is that those who read about my spiritual pilgrimage will find the inspiration they need to explore their inner selves and seek out their own quiet moments and holy places where they can experience transformation.

— James A. Belcher
2001

# PART 1

# Vigils

# Lounging on a Deserted Beach

*There is perpetual mystery and
excitement in living on the seashore.*
—Gavin Maxwell

When my family and I moved to Pensacola, Florida, I was less than excited about the prospect of living near the beach. I was not a beach person. I took no pleasure in high humidity, the broiling sun, and sticky winds that lacerated my back with sand. I thought of myself as a mountain man, at home among the birch-covered hills that rose out of shaded valleys, their peaks hidden in a soupy mist.

The ocean proved a seductive temptress. After spending so many sunny days lounging on her white sand, I became the beach bum I once viewed with contempt. The washing of ocean waves now lulls me into a state of gentle, peaceful tranquility. The barren horizon offers a welcome alternative to an artificial world of air-conditioned, high-rise buildings. The haunting cry of the sea gull echoes against something lonely and eternal in my soul. That is why, early on this Friday morning in May, I find myself drawn to these sugar white shores.

The hour reads eight o'clock. Already the Florida sun beats with the intensity of approaching summer. Fifteen minutes earlier a thick layer of dark gray clouds, similar to thunderheads in their appearance, blanketed the eastern sky. The sun resembled a blurred yellow disk peeping from behind a curtain of haze as a drifting fog passed between it and the earth. Above the horizon, where time meets eternity, the threatening clouds gave way to a passion pink skyline streaked with purple. But now the quiet glory of early morning flees and the temperature climbs.

The beach is deserted this morning except for a flock of sea gulls. The gulls watch me with eager eyes as I unfold my lounge chair. They scurry over to where I sit. Their open throats and familiar cries tell me they hope I brought them breakfast. When the birds see I have no bread crumbs to give them, they waddle away to pursue communal rituals. I lie back in my chair and let the radiance of a new day soak into my weary spirit.

The older I grow and the greater the amount of energy my vocation requires from me, the more I need deserted places like the beach at early morning. I need to be away from people with their unrealistic expectations and constant demands. I need to remain motionless for a few hours while listening to the surf crashing against the shore. I need to feel the easy, warming sun against my back and plant my bare feet in the cool sand. I need to close my eyes and lose myself in the salty odor of a beach breeze. Something about this ritual of separation infuses new life into my worn soul.

The progression of our lives over the years intrigues me. Each of us charts a course we sense promises us fulfillment. We start out on our life journeys thinking our efforts will change the world. A few years down the road we realize we are not going to change society, in spite of our frantic activity, so we modify our ambitions; we settle for changing the people around us. Eventually we discover we cannot control even the people closest to us, at which point we surrender the idealistic dreams of youth. We shift our focus to more self-centered ambitions—the acquisition of money, success and power.

Most of us waste too many of our brief years chasing the clay-footed gods of secularism. As the strain of time begins to weigh heavily on our souls, we recognize the fallacy of this kind of existence. That recognition becomes the point where we find ourselves drawn to lonely places like this beach—places where status and success do not seem so important, places where feelings of rush and hurry give way to serenity, places where we find the space to sit and ruminate without interruption. The deep things of life happen not when we are in the crowd, but when we are alone.

Perhaps this is why the ocean is so seductive. Maybe this is why I find myself drawn to her on this pleasant Friday morning. The ocean purifies my soul. The beach renews my spirit.

# Sitting on a Park Bench
# in the Fog

*The highest and most decisive
experience is to be alone.*

—Carl Jung

The black chronograph on my wrist reads ten minutes after seven o'clock. Today marks the third consecutive morning our seaside community has experienced fog. This fog seems to be a dry fog—dense, heavy, and low-hanging. Being engulfed in this kind of fog is like being wrapped in a ball of cotton. I have lived in Pensacola for seven years and have seen nothing like this trio of foggy mornings. Even the airport was socked in for several hours the day before yesterday.

Being caught up in a foggy day feels to me like being nestled in an old favorite blanket. The fog holds me within itself; it comforts me and helps me feel secure. I like the sensation of feeling hidden that comes when the fog rolls in off the bay. That is why this morning I find myself perched on a comfortable wooden bench in Pensacola's historic Seville Square, surrounded by hundred-year-old buildings, live oak trees, and a carpet of winter grass sprinkled with dead leaves. The old gazebo across the sidewalk stands silent. The swings where children play on spring afternoons sit empty and motionless. My only companion is an imitation turn-of-the-century gas streetlamp keeping vigil over a half-full trash barrel.

Seville Square greets few visitors this gray February morning. A transient scours the garbage cans for breakfast. An executive wearing a blue suit and swinging a brief case from his left hand scurries to work along the brick sidewalk. The bar across the street shut its doors hours ago, although when the wind blows from the north, I can still smell the sour odor of stale beer mixed with cigarette smoke.

Sitting here, hidden in the mist that engulfs this peaceful quarter, kindles the reflective aspect of my personality. I consider how strange it is that I should find myself in this quaint hamlet. Of all the highways and byways and country lanes I have traveled in my life, how did I arrive at this tiny speck on the globe called Pensacola? Like so many wandering souls immersed in this rootless culture, my occupation brought me here.

My occupation. My vocation. My calling. It is hard to believe I have been in the trenches of pastoral ministry for more than twenty-five years. Without my being aware of it, pages have fallen from the calendar like autumn leaves from the towering oaks that surround me. These days I feel the chronic ache of advancing age more than the vitality of youth. I sense the routine of the daily grind more than the thrill of serving God. I suspect that's why I enjoy losing myself in thick fogs and deserted parks. At middle age, when I imagine I should have more to contribute to the world than ever before, I find myself less willing to speak.

Ezra Pound comes to mind. Pound wrote and lectured for most of his life. He stood on center stage in the glare of the spotlight. In his later years Pound retreated into silence, saying little even to family and friends. Ezra Pound's silence was self-criticism against his former public life. It is too bad that the aging poet lapsed into silence in his twilight years. He could have spoken more profoundly during the latter period of his life than at any previous time.

That is the way some of us feel about our noisy existences. We grow weary of the chatter. We get tired of hearing our own voices. We become disgusted with the grasping and clutching of a greedy society. We recognize that our helter-skelter activity was little more than chasing the wind. And so we fade into silence. The older I grow, the more I require silence in my life. That is why I will sit here on this bench for a few more minutes and pray that the fog does not lift.

# Listening to the Coffee Perk

*All the evils of life have fallen upon us because men will not sit alone quietly in a room.*

—Blaise Pascal

The alarm clock next to my bed reads five o'clock. I stumble along a darkened hallway into the den and grope for the cord to the window blinds. My fingers do not seem to work in this semi-conscious state between sleep and wakefulness. With an awkward motion I draw the floor-length, almond-colored shutters to one side and survey a sleeping world. Darkness melts into darkness as the quiet room blends with the silent woods and black winter sky.

I will not turn on the television this morning. I cannot endure the coarse vulgarity of yesterday's news, nor another automobile salesman screaming in my ear. The world becomes louder, more shallow, and less relevant with each passing year. I cannot tolerate its intrusion into my waking moments. I will give an ear to its bedlam and an audience to its surging throng when the sun climbs into the sky. For the moment I want to sit in the darkness, listen to the silence, and watch the stillness.

The rhythmic sound of coffee perking in the kitchen catches my ear. In my five decades of life I cannot recall sitting and listening to the coffee pot grumble. I have heard the click and clatter of coffee perking as a background noise while I considered more important matters, but this morning is the first time I have paid attention to it with the ear of my soul. There is a sonorous peacefulness in the perking melody of a coffee pot. Who would have guessed that such a common household staple as coffee would provide a rich background for contemplation?

Contemplation comes from the Latin word meaning *abiding within the temple*. This morning finds me abiding in the temple with God. This silent room is the temple and a mug of coffee becomes the sacrament. Perhaps our inner selves would grow more resonant and full-flavored if we listened more often to the coffee brewing.

The hands on the clock over the kitchen table turn past six o'clock. With regret I must leave my silent realm, this holy place that nurtures my spirit. The universe beyond these silent walls lies shadowy and motionless; but when it wakes and I encounter it in an hour, the day will find more than enough tasks to keep me busy.

# Enjoying the Solitude before Dawn

*Among all our good people, not one in a thousand sees the sun rise once in a year. They know nothing of the morning.*

—Daniel Webster

Following an unsettling dream, I rouse myself from sleep at three o'clock in the morning. Unable to fall back into slumber, I crawl from the bed to begin my day. I do not feel well this morning. I am not ill, but have the unpleasant sensation that some diminutive cog or wheel inside my body is spinning around faster than it should. My stomach grumbles and I feel a burning sensation in my chest. I recall the extravagant meal Ella and I consumed last night at the steak house. Friday is the night Ella and I go out to dinner. The ritual is a simple way of celebrating the fact we have survived another week. As I sit here in the darkness of my den eight hours later, I remind myself to exercise more discipline the next time we go to a restaurant.

My thoughts during these quiet moments before dawn focus on my spiritual life as well as my physical existence. I recall the daylight hours of the previous day—time I spent alone reading, writing, meditating, and praying. I found renewal in the solitude. The silence spoke in soothing tones to my weary soul.

I ruminate on the aging author Doris Grumbach who, in 1994, spent fifty days alone in her cabin on the coast of Maine. She relates her solitary adventure in her book *Fifty Days of Solitude*. Grumbach chose the dead of winter for her sojourn into silence. She watched the snow pile up around her house. She read and wrote and occasionally watched a video. Silence and stillness became her companions. When Grumbach ended her self-imposed exile, she returned to the world of people with a depth and a clarity she had not possessed before her retreat.

Each time I embrace solitude—for an hour, a day, or a week—I feel emotions welling up within me similar to those Grumbach describes in her book. In solitude I feel holy, pure, and noble. I realize a tranquility otherwise hidden. In solitude I discover that God has something for me to do with my life other than what I have done with it over the last five decades. I cannot define God's unfolding purpose for my life. No doors of opportunity open for me. No lights come on in my consciousness. But in my solitary moments, I encounter a depth of existence not encountered in the busy moments. I sense that God wants me to enter into this silence so that I can speak about it to the world.

The clock tells me dawn approaches. I hear the first bird as it announces the coming day. A dull gray light creeps through the kitchen window. I will pour a second cup of coffee, turn off the lamp that illuminates my note pad, and listen to the dying silence for a few more minutes.

# Studying before Daybreak

*Every time I go out among men,*
*I return less a man.*

—St. Augustine

Five o'clock. Daybreak lingers for another hour. The house lies hushed and dark. Ella prefers the seclusion of the bedroom this morning, covers tucked around her chin, knees drawn into a semi-fetal position. In a few moments she will stumble sleepily into the kitchen and pour a cup of coffee; the rich aroma of vanilla hazelnut already wafts through the house. David and Matthew slumber peacefully in their beds; the scattered piles of dirty jeans, socks, and sweatshirts that litter their rooms do not bother them.

I am not fully awake as I sit here in this old green reclining chair in the den. I lean my head against the chair's back and close my eyelids. The soft gray carpet cradles my bare feet. I yearn to drift into sleep for just one more hour.

To my left a wall of varnished pine bookcases adorned with the usual family articles—pictures, trophies, and books—catches my attention. I detect the outline of the Childcraft my mother gave me for Christmas when I was four years old. When David and Matt were toddlers they crawled onto my lap, clutching one of the orange volumes in their pudgy hands, and squealed, "Read, Daddy! Please read!" David and Matt are growing up now and are no longer interested in what an aging parent has to say. To my right stands an empty fireplace bordered by a raised brick hearth. An assortment of martial arts trophies, too tall to fit on the bookshelves, stands on the hearth next to the fireplace. The trophies are legacies from my younger days when beating an opponent to the punch seemed to be the most important thing in life.

The hands on the wall clock slowly sweep toward six. The pale ash of dawn timidly creeps through the large sliding glass door that looks out over the back yard. The first faint flicker of light filters into the room. From the soft glow of a lamp over my shoulder, I reflect on the notes tucked between the pages of my Bible. Two hours from now I will stand in the public arena and grapple for the right words as I share my faith in Christ with the men's prayer breakfast. A host of servers will swish from kitchen to table carrying an assortment of bacon, eggs, grits, biscuits, orange juice, and coffee. Conversation and laughter will roll easily from everyone's lips. Now in these quiet moments I sit alone, secluded from the prying eyes of the world, observed only by God.

The older I grow, the more comfortable I become resting in God's presence. I am coming to understand that I do not have to be perfect to win God's love; God accepts me as I am. God is the Creator who fashioned my soul and who knew me before my birth, when I existed in my mother's womb. God sustains my body and my soul as I journey through life. God gives meaning to each chapter of my earthly existence.

My attention again turns from personal thoughts to the sermon notes that lay in my lap. I reflect on my spiritual fathers, my mentors in the faith, who arose early to greet the sun and conquer the challenges each morning brought. Abraham got up early on the day God rained judgment on Sodom and Gomorrah; the old patriarch fled to his altar and prayed for the redemption of his people. Moses awakened early when he went before Pharaoh to command the mighty king of Egypt to release the Hebrew slaves. Joshua met the sunrise before he led the Israelites across the Jordan River into the Promised land. Gideon, anxious to learn if the children of Israel would defeat the Midianites, rushed from his bed in the darkness to check the fleece he had thrown out to God.

Jesus awakened in the silence of the night, got out

of bed, and journeyed alone into the Galilean hills to listen for the voice of the heavenly Father. The Gospel of Mark records, "And in the morning, a great while before day, he rose and went out to a lonely place, and there he prayed" (Mk. 1:35).

The women who served Jesus during his public ministry rushed to the tomb at daybreak after the crucifixion to anoint Jesus's body with spices. Matthew writes, "Now after the Sabbath, toward the dawn of the first day of the week, Mary Magdalene and the other Mary went to see the sepulcher" (Mt. 28:11). Luke describes how the followers of Jesus made their way to the temple as the sun peeped over the Judean hills: "they entered the temple at daybreak and taught" (Acts 5:21).

At last the morning sun bathes my private sanctuary with rays of dazzling white brilliance. My ear catches the sound of water running in the shower. I glance once more at the notes I have scribbled on index cards. The words of Bail Pennington, the monk of Gethsemani, catch my eye: "At such an hour what does creation do but await the sun? What can we do but await the Son?" I greet the day, comforted by the assurance that the God who accompanied his servants thousands of years ago will go with me through all the responsibilities I must shoulder in the coming hours.

# Keeping Vigil on
# Friday Morning

*I have a strange longing for the
great simple primeval things,
such as the sea....*

—Oscar Wilde

The hour reads fifteen minutes until seven o'clock. I find myself drawn to the beach on this gray, windswept October morning. Today is the first Friday I have made this pilgrimage in many months. I have been away from this holy place too long.

I feel compelled to run on this lonely occasion. This urge to push myself beyond a walking pace is the first I have felt since last spring; and so I jog easily along the two-mile stretch of road that takes me from the Johnson Beach pavilion to the turnaround circle and back. The route is a strenuous four-mile workout for someone like me who is no longer in peak physical condition.

The early fall sky is laden with deep blue thunderheads. I cannot escape their silent threat as I jog slowly, surveying my quiet world. The ominous clouds hang like blankets suspended from the heavens by invisible wires. Their hue, somewhere between blue and black, creates a distinct line of demarcation where the sky meets the green-tinted gulf on the distant horizon. The sea cannot make up its mind if it wants to nurse its anger or give itself up to a tranquil state of meditation.

I feel comfortable in this lonely environment where the world ends and eternity begins. I am drawn like iron to a magnet to these desolate sands, uninhabited this day by even the herons.

A mile into my solitary jaunt, two runners, a man and a woman, moving at a faster pace than my relaxed gait, ease past me on my right. They appear to be in their early thirties. The comfortable manner in which they fit together tells me they have loved one another long beyond the honeymoon. "Great day!" I call as they go by on the opposite side of the road.

"Great day for running!" one shouts in response.

"Wonderful day for joggers and poets!" I tell myself as the pair's brisk strides take them beyond earshot toward a distant sand dune.

Once again I am left alone in my isolated world

of thought. There was a day when I would have challenged them for the lead. This day I am happy to let my aging legs propel me along the course. I do not mind growing older and slower. Aging brings its own unique rewards—the death of youthful compulsions, the birth of wisdom and reflection, the courage to think for oneself instead of going along with the mindless herd. I find no quarrel with this juncture I am reaching in my journey through life. I am content to run my own race. I do not need any more trophies to collect dust. I will leave the finish line to the winners.

The ocean lies within sight on both sides as I glide over this skinny finger of land. The ocean is so much more than water and waves washing against soggy sand. The ocean is infinity in full view of the human eye. If humanity could explore the ocean's hidden depths, we would discover mysteries more intriguing than the pock-marked surface of the moon that fascinates us so much. The ocean urges me to explore the bottomless wonder of my soul. However, it seems the deeper I probe, the more confusing the murky waters become.

So, this morning, I content myself with admiring surface things. I feel the salty sting of beach wind on my face. I tune my ear to the surging tide. I warm to the chill of this lonely fall morning. I feel the glory of living mixed with the agony of aging as my lungs struggle to take each breath. When the unseen finish line comes into view, I hope to die with my running shoes on.

# At a Sidewalk Cafe

*In silence the scattered pieces of my
life fall into place, and I see again
where I am going.*

—Susan Muto

The eight o'clock hour finds me perched in a comfortable chair at a sidewalk cafe three blocks from my office. From a Parisian's perspective, the nearby four-lane artery with its bustling shopping center does not qualify as a quaint boulevard. Neither does this bagel shop meet the standards of a cozy coffeehouse. In this accelerated American culture of gas-guzzling automobiles and cookie-cutter housing tracts, a plastic table on a busy street corner is the best one can expect.

My solitude comes in diminishing doses these days, like this slowed-down half-hour where I nurse a cup of decaf and watch the morning sun burn away the fog. I enjoy foggy mornings. Fog invites me to pause for a few extra minutes before jumping headlong into the day's overcrowded schedule. It beckons me to sit quietly for awhile and let my imagination play.

My thoughts on this foggy morning turn to my father. Five months ago the family learned Dad had Alzheimer's disease. Since I was Dad's only child, caring for him became my responsibility. It was a responsibility I assumed willingly. I had heard horror stories of how Alzheimer's patients gradually lost their mental faculties and how, in the final stages of the disease, they no longer recognized the persons closest to them. Since I had not seen my father often during the previous eight years, I wanted to make the most of the dwindling opportunities we had left to be together.

Between July, when I learned of Dad's illness, and November, I went to see him as frequently as my overloaded schedule permitted. The two of us sat on the porch of the nursing facility where he lived. We watched the green leaves of summer fade to gold, release their tenacious grips on life, and fall silently to the ground. When lunchtime came we headed for a nearby steak house. With grief I observed how Dad's once robust appetite had withered to little more than a few spoonfuls of ice cream. After lunch we drove leisurely through the countryside. Even when he was young, Dad enjoyed riding slowly along winding back roads; the drives were therapeutic for his restless spirit.

Those drives through the countryside gave Dad and I the time and space we needed to talk. Sometimes our conversations focused on trivial matters; we chattered about old times and people from our past. Other times we discussed more pressing issues, like the stipulations of Dad's will and his granting me power of attorney over his business affairs. During the serious conversations I was glad driving required me to fasten my gaze on the highway.

On an overcast afternoon in October, Dad broached the subject of his illness. He informed me his short term memory was fading rapidly. We had just finished a basket of chicken fingers when he brought up the issue. I humorously replied, "If your memory is failing, you probably don't remember those catfish we just ate." Dad chuckled, and so did I. Laughter helped to lighten the somber moments.

Dad and I put the ribbon around our package on an Indian summer morning in November. He told me he did not want any heroic life-sustaining measures taken when he came to the moment of death. He wanted to slip quietly and with dignity into the eternal life which awaited. Dad affirmed his love for me, a love in which I had felt secure since childhood. With a gentleness in his voice I never remember hearing, Dad told me I was the finest son any father could have. He said he was proud of me and my accomplishments. I held his hand, stroked his once powerful arm, and replied, "I love you, Dad. You're the best father any son could want." He died two days later. I buried him in the family plot next to my grandmother in the little town where both of us had spent the carefree days of boyhood.

On this foggy morning three weeks after Dad's funeral, I sense my own existence coming full circle. At the age of forty-nine, I have more years behind me than ahead of me. Most of the people I love have moved on in one way or another. Dad is dead. Mom continues to grow older in spite of her vigorous lifestyle. Ella, the bride of my youth, finds herself in her productive years and spends most of her days teaching fourth graders their multiplication tables. Our oldest lives two-thousand miles away. He has found his niche as a construction worker and dotes on his one-year-old daughter, my grandchild whom I have not yet seen. Our youngest attends college ten hours from home and spends his semester breaks hanging out with friends and playing volleyball on the beach.

With each passing year my thoughts return to the affirmation of the Psalmist: "Lord thou hast been our dwelling place in all generations. Before the mountains were brought forth, or ever thou hadst formed the earth and the world, from everlasting to everlasting thou art God (Ps. 90:1-2)."

I find comfort in the assurance that all of us live and die in the hands of a loving God.

# Watching the River Flow

*Tired at last, he sat on the bank, while
the river chattered on to him, a
babbling procession of the best stories
in the world.*

—Kenneth Grahame

I sit on a rock watching the gently rushing waters of
the Chattahoochee River as it runs through Helen,
Georgia. Helen is a small hamlet of some 300 persons
in the north Georgia mountains. The town was
drying up like a riverbed during a southern drought
until the late 1960's. That's when its citizens came up
with the idea of transforming their decaying buildings into an authentic Alpine village.

These days the streets of Helen bustle with

trinket shops, candy kitchens, sausage and sauerkraut restaurants. Minivans packed with whimpering children and frustrated parents creep bumper-to-bumper along Helen's Main Street every day from morning until sundown. Parking spots go for premium prices. A fudge vendor who has lived here all her life told me the traffic congestion was her biggest complaint following Helen's renaissance. Helen, Georgia, is not Ischgl, Austria; but for American tourists without enough time and money to visit the real thing, it will suffice.

While I enjoy the excited stir of downtown Helen, I also need large amounts of elbow room. That is why I find myself perched on a flat boulder this morning gazing into the waters of the Chattahoochee. The river seems to be the most tranquil spot around. Even here, there are too many fishermen to suit my solitary tastes. Fishermen live under the mistaken impression that rivers were made for fishing; they have not realized that rivers are for poets and romantics, for people who enjoy sunrises and sunsets.

An hour from now this nearly-deserted body of water will teem with tubers—kids and adolescents and adults on yellow, blue, and green inner tubes—all trying to stay cool in the Georgia summer. Even as I jot down these thoughts, shuttle buses from the Cool River Tubing Company deliver loads of animated vacationers to the put-in point several miles north of town. I prefer sitting here alone, watching the water bubble along the rocky bottom, listening to the continuous rush of rapids, and feeling the cold rock beneath me. This river has a peaceful quality about it. It is soothing to the tormented spirit. It causes one to ponder the meaning of life.

At the risk of losing myself in too much philosophy, I consider how all of our lives resemble a trip down the river. We have our put-in point. Life begins at a clearly defined moment, and pushes us on to an unseen destination. Sometimes the journey moves slowly; other times, rapidly. Like the stages of this river, there are serene spots and swirling eddies. There are rocky places, too. Even when we sit motionless, we somehow continue inching our way toward the vast, eternal gulf.

As I think back on my own trip, I am struck by the notion that I choose not to retrace a single stage of my five decades of travel. The waters of my existence have run too deep and too rough. The rocks have proven too jagged and the whirlpools too engulfing. There have been too few refreshing pools, too few shady spots. I am weary of fighting the current; I need to drift for awhile.

Like every river traveler, I cannot see around the upcoming bend; but I sense myself feeling cautiously optimistic about approaching it. I trust that God, who has accompanied me this far on the journey, will keep me afloat through whatever rapids and falls lie ahead. I feel confident God will lead me to the peaceful backups my soul requires.

The Psalmist writes, "He leads me beside quiet waters" (Ps. 23:2). I appreciate the New International

Version's rendering of the text, and I like its emphasis on quiet. As we run the river of life, God steers us through smooth and choppy waters. The important thing is not the kind of waters through which we pass—shallow or deep, rushing or gurgling. What matters is the assurance that God travels with us.

# Reflecting on
# a Good Ride

*But right now I'll just sit here*
*contentedly and watch the river flow.*
— Bob Dylan

I find myself drawn to the river again this morning and have chosen a different spot for silent reflection. The waters that gurgle past me have not changed. They remain as cool and peaceful, as soothing to the soul as ever. This wooden bench with its tilted backrest affords a degree of comfort I did not find in my former perch on the rock.

Beneath my feet the amber water rushes under a European-style stone bridge and washes into white foam against the boulders that rise from the riverbed.

I am struck by how clearly I can detect the currents as they plunge full force against the rocks, then veer left and right, claiming the course of least resistance. This shady spot along the Chattahoochee is a pleasant place to sit and while away the morning. I am alone except for the rapids. The only sound I hear is the rushing of the waterfalls. I am content to surrender to the serenity this pastoral setting offers.

As I think about these unhurried moments, I become acutely aware that this morning is different from most mornings in my life. Like so many millions of others, I belong to the nameless, faceless working class who wakes to an alarm clock and grabs a quick shower before rushing out the door. Unlike others—save other parish clergy— the majority of my days fill up with things I never planned to do. The Christian mystic Evelyn Underhill describes our years when she writes, "We spend most of our lives conjugating three verbs: to Want, to Have, and to Do." I find little time to sit in the shade, listen to the river, and study the sprinkling of late summer leaves that lose their grip and drift in a spiral pattern into the surging waters.

Ten years ago, when the desire for silence and solitude began to take root in my soul, I found myself resentful of the demands that forced me into a chaotic existence and denied me the quiet fruits of meditation. I railed against the helter-skelter dimensions that characterized my years. Anger was part of the process—an early stage in the journey—a section of the river I had to travel. But at this point in time, ten years downstream, I find myself beyond most of the bitterness. I am learning the wisdom of Thomas á Kempis: "Seek a secret place, love to dwell alone, desire the conversation of none; but rather pour out devout prayer to God."

In these mid-life years I am learning to ask God for silence when I feel overworked rather than lashing out at God because my schedule is hectic. I am learning to accept the fact that I can enter solitude only on isolated occasions and that most of the time I must make myself available to the people in my care. While my life continues at a too-active pace to take, I no longer feel the bitterness of a rebellious heart. During some unrecognized moment I realized my years are not my own. My life does not belong to me. It has not belonged to me since that hot June night thirty years ago when, sitting around the campfire at a Methodist Church camp, I surrendered my life to Jesus Christ. Since that evening my life has belonged to other people—to God, to my family, and to those persons God calls me to serve. I accept the necessity of living for God instead of living for myself and of paying more attention to the divine voice than to my inward desire.

My ruminations are interrupted by a group of tubers floating leisurely down the river. They appear to be a family on summer break from the office, the classroom, the kitchen—from wherever their busy schedules take them most days. The mom and dad look to be around thirty-five. Mom has blonde hair. Dad is slender and balding. Two young children, a boy and a girl, accompany them on bright yellow tubes. I notice Mom has a secure grip on the youngest child's hand. I understand her parental insecurity. Life has a way of snatching away the people and things we cherish; we must maintain a tight hold. The five of us exchange pleasant greetings, and I ask Dad if they are having a good ride. We banter briefly before the easy current sweeps them downstream. As the four tubers drift out of sight, I ponder how all of us are trying to do what Mom, Dad, and the kids are doing. We are all trying to have a good ride.

A few weeks ago I officiated at the funeral of an 87-year-old widow. She and her husband remained lovers more than fifty years. The two of them square-danced, sang in the church choir, and raised four sons. As her oldest son and I sat in the cardiac care waiting room, sensing his mother's inevitable death, he commented, "She had a good ride!"

The important issue is not how slowly or swiftly the river runs, nor how long the journey takes—but whether or not we make it a good ride. I pray God will rescue me from the rapids and grant me a pleasurable trip, perhaps in some secluded forest by a peacefully flowing river.

*Part 2*

# Pilgrimages

# Hiking the
# Appalachian Trail

*Surrounded by hours of moving we*
*find a moment of quiet stillness.*

— Henri Nouwen

Our party of eight makes its way across Fontana Dam, due south of the Great Smoky Mountain National Park. We are eight strangers from different parts of the globe, bound together by a common purpose. We will spend the day hiking the Appalachian Trail. Bruk serves as our guide. Bruk is a young fellow in his early twenties, slender and sinewy, with blond hair hanging to his shoulders. Bruk recently earned his bachelor's degree in cultural anthropology and plans to do graduate work in the fall at the University of

Tennessee. He is an experienced camper and back-packer, having hiked extensively in Australia and Borneo before returning to the United States to trek the Appalachian Trail. Bruk commenced his Appalachian adventure at Springer Mountain in Georgia, the trail's southern terminus. He made his way as far as Fontana before running out of money, which explains why he signed on as a Fontana Village trail guide for the summer.

Bruk is everything I would like to be, but never will be—wanderer, explorer, adventurer, Bohemian, unattached to middle-class values. Our group jokes and laughs as we make our way across the dam. We are filled with anticipation at the wilderness experience that lies ahead, as well as with awe at the massive concrete structure beneath our feet. We pause briefly to snap photos and peer over the metal railing at the river hundreds of feet below. A quarter of a mile from Fontana Dam, the concrete roadway surrenders to a narrow, rocky, root-studded path that winds back and forth up the steep mountain. Bruk explains that this portion of the famous corridor from Georgia to Maine is the steepest section in the Smoky Mountain Park. I bring up the rear of the single file safari and quickly fall behind the other hikers. In spite of my being a seasoned runner and walker, I cannot keep up with the younger, more experienced trail hikers. My heart pounds and my lungs heave during the severe climb. The water bottles in my pack feel like bricks. I question my decision to sign on to this all-day excursion. The pace slows as we make our way up the tortuous mountain. I find relief in the frequent rest stops, as well as in the discovery that the other hikers' breaths seem as labored as mine. We are in a world protected from the blight of modern humanity. It is the world of the black bear, bobcat, fox, and deer. It is a world of oak, birch, and even a few young, not-yet-diseased American chestnut trees; a world of blueberries and huckleberries that have never felt the withering spray of pesticides; a world of rocky overlooks and breath-taking views. Pleasures are simple in this primitive environment—like plucking a handful of blueberries and letting their sweet juice play on your tongue; sitting on a rock beneath a spreading oak and watching the sky unfold as far as the clear blue of eternity; basking in a friendly sun, the heat generating a damp sweat, then entering the cooling shade of dense woods.

The sun passes high noon. We approach our destination of Shuckstack Tower, located at the summit of the mountain. Shuckstack is an old fire tower used by the park service to spot forest blazes. Shuckstack Tower still is climbable; it is still maintained. The tower was abandoned long ago as an observation post. Satellite surveillance and other sophisticated monitoring devices proved more efficient. Electronic detection may be better for spotting forest fires than a pair of binoculars in an aging fire tower, but as I climb this holdover from the past, I realize that it alone can let me feel the wind on my face. It alone can offer a soul-stirring panorama, can draw me into the silence at the top of God's world.

Lunch is simple, like the world around me. A bottle of water. An apple. A handful of cranberry cookies. Hidden from full view by the bushes, a copperhead snake suns itself a couple of feet from the rock on which I eat my noonday meal. Neither of us poses a threat to the other as long as we are left undisturbed to soak in the midday sun. Our respite ended, the group continues the long journey which eventually will take us home. Before this day in the Smoky Mountains draws to a close, we will walk fifteen miles. Our bodies will know it: feet will blister, legs will throb, heads will pound. But we will find fulfillment in the agony because we have done more than simply hike a trail. We have touched something primitive within ourselves. We have discovered that mystical element which flickers in every heart, that spark which is the essence of life, which transforms mere existence into meaningful living. For one brief day we fanned that flicker into a flame.

# Hiking the
# Wolf Ridge Trail

*The clearest way into the universe is
through a forest wilderness.*

— John Muir

Our group of eight hikers takes a much-needed break
from our excursion on the Appalachian Trail. The time
is midafternoon. By this point in the day-long trek
we have become more than a group of strangers; we
have become a family. We have journeyed toward the
same destination; we have struggled up the same
mountainous inclines; we have shared the pain of sore
muscles and blistered feet; we have shouldered each
others' burdens. These experiences have forged a
familial bond that transcends the loose connections

implicit in a mere grouping. In the shade of this mountainside oasis, some of us slip the packs from our backs and plop against a fallen tree. Others kneel on their hands and knees and pore over a map. We have reached a crossroads in our adventure. Two choices confront us. We can take the old fire trail, the short route back to Twenty Mile Ranger Station; or we can strike out along the Wolf Ridge Trail. The fire trail will take an hour off of the exhausting journey. The route has a strong appeal to our sore feet and flagging spirits. The fire trail will be muddy. Wolf Ridge will take us several miles farther than the shorter route; but the scenery along Wolf Ridge makes the extra effort worthwhile.

As the group ponders its decision, I unzip my pack and take a long drink of the now tepid water I have been hauling since shortly after dawn. I think of how so many of my life experiences, like this hiking expedition, have brought me to personal crossroads. I have stood at too many intersections trying to decide which path to take. Many times I have chosen the wrong road. I have made some bad decisions and hurt too many people during the course of my life's journey; I am filled with remorse. I wonder where the years would have led me had I traveled a different route.

I am unsure why the group chooses to take the longer, more difficult route. Maybe we are gluttons for punishment. Perhaps no one wants to be the first to admit he or she is exhausted. After a brief discussion, the vote is unanimous. We will strike out along the Wolf Ridge Trail. Within two dozen steps we find ourselves in a world that gives no hint of civilization, save that of the beaten path. In some spots even the trail is overgrown with waist-high plant life. Our eyes take in the same sights our ancestors and Native Americans saw hundreds of years earlier with one exception. Notes our guide Bruk, "Four hundred years ago, giant American chestnut trees grew in this forest. They were wiped out by a European blight brought by the white man." A twinge of silent regret gently sweeps my soul as Bruk explains the saga of the American chestnut. I like chestnuts. I enjoy the sweet, juicy, yellow meat. I warm to the feelings and memories chestnuts conjure up within me. Some of the most peaceful moments of my boyhood were spent with a friend in his chestnut orchard. We carefully dug the nuts out of the prickly burrs; some-times our fingers bled. We were children; and as we ate, we spoke of life and hopes and dreams. Then my friend moved away. Someone else bought the house and allowed the little grove of well-pruned trees to die of neglect. Times change.

Our party walks in silence now, mostly from fatigue. We find ourselves too tired to carry on conversation. Most of us seek our own solitary space as each falls fifteen to twenty yards behind the hiker ahead. I bring up the end of the line, glad to be alone for a few minutes, feeling no hurry to catch up. The Wolf Ridge Trail crosses the same rushing river in several locations. At one crossing there are no stepping stones. We take off our shoes and socks and wade through the icy water. The chill refreshes my hot, aching feet. At other junctions, the river cascades over gray boulders before dropping five to ten feet. At some of the crossings we find a log laid across the gorge, top side sawed-off to create a smooth walking surface. I am moved by the majesty of this spattering river as it splashes and sprays its way from the mountain peak to the valley. If I were alone, I would pause by the river for a few minutes and sit on the rocks—and think—and listen—and pray. I am not alone. So I push on, pondering the words Jesus spoke to the woman of Samaria: "Everyone who drinks of this water will thirst again, but whoever drinks of the water that I shall give him will never thirst; the water that I shall give him will become in him a spring of water welling up to eternal life (John 4:13-14)."

As refreshing as this mountain stream is, as breathtaking as its cascading waters are, there is a spring of water that is more refreshing and awe-inspiring. That spring is the presence of God's Spirit, the Holy Spirit, within our hearts. I am drawn to the spring of water within me even more strongly than I am drawn to this river that tumbles and falls through these dense woods. The afternoon grows late. My watch tells me the time is past four o'clock. Thunder rumbles through the rapidly darkening forest. One peal sounds, then another. And still another, reverberating between the mountains, creating a continuous bellow. We find ourselves caught in one of the thunderstorms that pelts this part of the world on summer days. We listen in silence to the rain dancing on the canopy of leaves and limbs overhead; but the forest is so dense only a few droplets drip through to sprinkle us. Suddenly, without warning, the silent and winding trail that tantalized us for so much of the day disappears into a heavily traveled clay road. I take a final, longing glance toward the river that, like a friend, rejuvenated my sagging spirit; and once more I find myself trapped in the snare of civilization.

# Hiking the
# Pine Mountain Trail

*The solitary life is the life of one
drawn by the Father into the wilderness to be nourished by no other
spiritual food than Jesus.*

— Thomas Merton

The Pine Mountain Trail twists and turns for twenty-
three miles among the west Georgia hills. It
crisscrosses lonely highways where traffic seldom
ventures. It wanders in and out of evergreen
thickets. The Pine Mountain Trail, with its rustic
campsites, scenic overlooks, and hidden beauty,
provides the perfect getaway for persons who need

to escape the clamor of the world for a few hours or even several days. I hear the call of this footpath and the wild domain which nestles it. The call is soft yet compelling, whispered but distinct. It is the call of silent woods, gentle streams, and unruffled ponds. It is the invitation of the lover who understands her beloved's most intimate yearnings and replies, "Come. Enter my solitude. Rest in my shadows. Turn your weary face to my morning sun."

In response to the trail's call, I fill my pack with the barest of essentials—water, a notebook, and a pen—and turn to greet my companion. I look out on a new day, a fresh moment, when I will find balm for my wounded soul and rebirth for my lethargic spirit. The awakening moments after dawn find me tramping in silence, uphill and downhill, along the winding dirt path. Pine straw crunches beneath my feet. I leap a gurgling brook; my boots sink into the soft, black mud. The icy water feels cold to my ankles; it slakes my soul's thirst. I saunter across an earthen dam that stands guard over a forgotten pond. The dingy pool appears undisturbed in its moss-covered stagnation. My ears detect the throaty croak of a bullfrog and the gentle splash of a turtle scurrying from its rock. As I journey along this sacred walkway, I exult in the exploration of my lover. Her beauty glows with the aura of holiness. Her sounds echo with a hush, the sighs of a world not fully awake. Her long, supple limbs reach low, intertwined in embrace, creating a bridal arch. I am in the divine cathedral. I feel nurtured and protected, caressed in the arms of God. Eventually the grating, mechanical sounds of civilization fall away. The dense foliage obscures an overbearing sun that steadily climbs toward the newly born day. The world remains a shadow. I am lost in a morning twilight. My blistered soul finds new life in the cool solitude. After several hours the chill of daybreak gives way to the rising humidity of midmorning. I push deeper into the stilled forest. The underbrush surrenders to massive granite outcrops. The rocks are cold, gray, and jagged, unyielding in their harshness. They jut from the hillsides like ancient dragons peering from darkened caves. Another moment and I find myself standing on the edge of a precipice, reaching out into miles of nothingness. Beauty and majesty and glory flood my heart. I stand in speechless wonder, overwhelmed by the handiwork of God.

It is midday now. Fatigue stalks my trail. I recline against a flat boulder. I pull a bottle of water from my pack and rejoice to be sitting at the King's banquet table. I offer a silent blessing to the God who renews my strength and restores my soul. Time loses all meaning as my eye follows a hawk through its majestic loops and dives. The world explodes into a collage of color—snowy clouds, blue canopy, black loam, green and brown all around. God is the artist; creation, God's canvas. People of faith speak about hearing the utterance of God, the voice of the infinite Almighty calling to finite humanity. The old prophet Elijah perceived the still, small whisper as he waited alone, listening and wondering, in the wilderness. As I sit in these silent woods, pen in hand, listening to the breeze whistle through oak and hickory limbs, I question what the voice of God sounds like in my life. God is the sound of crickets in the deep woods. God is the rustling of wind in the trees and the soft crash of a pine cone as it tumbles to the ground. God is a bubbling stream gracefully gliding over pebbles and silt. God is the robin singing and the leaves crackling. God is silence and stillness, peace and serenity, tranquility and quietude. God speaks in comforting tones which bring together the fragmented pieces of our lives. I know, for I have heard God's soft, melodious lilt in my ear. Here in this outdoor temple, God speaks sounds of solace to my bruised spirit. "Come to me, all who labor and are heavy laden, and I will give you rest" (Mt. 11:28). "Look at the birds of the air. Consider the lilies of the field" (Mt. 6:26, 28). The divine Comforter and eternal Lover cradles my soul. Again I breathe the breath of life.

# Hiking the
# Conecuh Trail

*Long live the weeds and the wilder-*
*ness yet.*

— Gerard Manley Hopkins

Danny and Becky Hiller began hiking trails two years ago. Danny once stood on the rim of the Grand Canyon and wondered what exciting adventures waited at the bottom. Two summers later, he and Becky signed on for a guided hike to the canyon floor. To whip themselves into shape for the grueling trek, Danny and Becky took up trail hiking. My wife Ella and I express interest, and they invite us to accompany them one sun-splashed spring morning. Our destination is a six-mile stretch of the Conecuh Trail, the name given to several walking paths cutting through the Conecuh National Forest in the Florida panhandle and south Alabama. The forest mostly consists of skinny, scraggy pine trees hiding scrub brush, broom sage, and marsh grass. The terrain is sprinkled with an abundance of lakes with names like Open Pond, Buck Pond, and Blue Lake. Alligators infest the swampy areas while rattlers and coral snakes slither through the fallen pine needles and tufts of wire grass.

We leave the Hillers' Chevy van at a public parking area adjacent to the soggy shores of Open Pond. While waiting for the other hikers to arrange their day packs, I gaze out across the placid waters, hoping to spot an alligator. Some years back, a lone bicyclist stopped for a cooling swim in Open Pond before continuing his sweaty trip across the countryside. A ten-foot bull gator chewed his left arm off at the shoulder. The victim survived, rescued by fishermen; the alligator was exterminated by the forest service. As the sun climbs to ten o'clock, with our packs adjusted to comfortable positions, the four of us ease onto the grassy footpath. The route is marked by diamond-shaped aluminum patches driven into tree trunks with large nails. The trio of hikers ahead of me walk in a cluster, talking and laughing. I join their banter to be sociable, but prefer the serenity of my primitive surroundings. Bringing up the rear of our group proves no problem for me since Danny enjoys leading. Danny Hiller is a good friend; he thinks deeply and speaks softly. Danny is a seasoned trail hiker; I trust his wilderness instincts. Within the span of fifteen minutes, I lapse into my natural state of silence.

From my vantage point thirty feet off the pace, I drink in the sights, sounds, and smells of this small section of God's vast, diverse world. My initial reaction to the Conecuh Trail is disappointment. I have explored wilderness far more scenic than the Conecuh Forest. I have hiked trails more rugged than this flat, grass-covered walkway. Hardwood forests with dense foliage, granite boulders, and steep climbs appeal to my personality more than this swampy path with its scrubby conifers and marsh grass withering under a semi-tropical sun. North Florida is my home during these middle years of my life, so I force myself to enjoy the area's landscape. An Everglades wilderness is more nurturing to me than the concrete jungles and asphalt roadways I traverse most days.

Somewhere beyond the second mile of the pilgrimage, our party of four approaches a creek overflowing its banks from two days of thunderstorms earlier in the week. The swollen river proves too wide for us to leap and too deep to trip across on the rocks. There is no footbridge. The only way to cross is to remove our shoes and socks and wade into the knee-deep, muddy slush. My memory automatically compares this stagnant ribbon of brown silt to the crystal rivers of the north country where icy water cascades over giant, moss-covered rocks creating Niagara-like waterfalls. Ten minutes beyond the creek, we reach the gurgling stream called Blue

Spring on the trail map. The map's colorful picture drawn in refreshing light blue exaggerates the beauty of the actual spring which proves to be more mosquito-infested than pastoral. We pause long enough to wipe the dried mud from between our toes and put on our shoes. A burning sun climbs to its mid-most point in the sky as we plod through the grassy wetlands. In some places we must tiptoe on the trail's edge to avoid rain-soaked bogs. We resemble children walking the rails along a deserted railroad track.

Conversation gives way to silence as it does on every adventure when weariness begins to set in. The silence proves fertile soil for rumination. I feel ashamed of my earlier critical thoughts about the Conecuh Trail. There is no place I enjoy spending my life more than in a stretch of wilderness. Wilderness haunts my soul. Yet I silently complained because the trees are pine instead of oak and the waters muddy rather than clear. I whisper a quiet prayer, asking God to forgive my lack of gratitude. As if to reinforce my need for repentance, our party winds around a bend in the trail where a breathtaking swamp unfolds its beauty before us. I stand in speechless wonder at acre upon acre of shallow, algae-coated water and marsh grass littered with dead, decaying stumps. Surely this must have been what creation resembled before time was measured and before humanity began to ravage, pillage, and plunder. This lost world, where dinosaurs once ruled and where modern men and women still tread cautiously, makes our sun-baked trek worth-while. I have observed nothing like this scene in the giant oak domains of the north country. For a second time I offer a silent prayer, this one of gratitude to the God who painted beauty into the raw land and gave me eyes to behold it.

A few more twists and turns in the trail bring Danny, Becky, Ella, and me back to the parking area where we began our hike. I settle into a swivel chair in the rear of the comfortable, air-conditioned van and munch on cheddar cheese, wheat crackers, and a crisp, sweet apple. I am surrounded by the goodwill of friends and nurtured by a God who speaks to me through creation. The journey home is pleasant.

# Walking the
# PARCOURSE

*When the pressure of our complex
city life thins my blood and benumbs
my brain, I seek relief in the trail.*
— Hamlin Garland

Sometimes a deep, aching abyss opens in my soul. There is no denying its awful presence. When I feel this spiritual fissure tearing into my life, nothing brings me comfort. I grow restless and discontented. An empty loneliness settles over me. Often this loneliness takes the form of a mild depression. I withdraw into myself and become quiet and reflective. I ponder, think, and ruminate, struggling to understand why my life must be this way. I wrestle with personal demons. In these painful moments, being with people brings little consolation. The presence of others unsettles me and adds to the heaviness that weighs on my spirit. There was a time when I begged God to fill this black hole that opens in my soul. I grew resentful toward God because he did not answer my prayers, but instead left me in my gut-wrenching pain. The longer I lived with this sense of incompleteness, the more I understood God could not heal my wounds. The sense of woundedness I felt so acutely was God within me. The pain, the emptiness, the bottomless void was a personal God living in my heart, creating within me a dissatisfaction with everything less than God. I realized that, when an individual has tasted God, even for one fleeting second, that person never will be satisfied with anything or anyone else—for everything else is less than God. What an incomprehensible paradox—to yearn so desperately for God, yet need to be healed from the terrifying sense of God's presence.

A week ago God again started rummaging in the cellar of my inner self. I would have been more comfortable had God remained asleep. Encounter with the divine is never easy. God chose not to sleep, or stay on vacation, or go wherever God goes during those periods when I find myself at home in the world. God stirred. And that is why this morning I must hike a lonely, wooded trail. The solitude of the forest, the mountains, the beach on a blustery day—these lonely places become balm to my hurting soul. My place of healing this day is the PARCOURSE.

PARCOURSE stands for Physical Activity and Recreation Course. The PARCOURSE is an eight-mile trail that winds through the Naval Air Station near our home in Pensacola. Laid out by the Navy for the physical conditioning of its recruits, the PARCOURSE is wide enough for two persons to walk shoulder-to-shoulder. Its edges are defined by railroad ties. In some places the trail is covered with sawdust and wood shavings. In other places the surface is composed of crushed seashells, gravel, pine straw, or beach sand. Unlike a secluded mountain trail which runs through vast expanses of woods without encountering civilization, the PARCOURSE is not entirely shielded from public view. It travels for several hundred yards parallel to a busy four-lane highway. It passes old Fort Barrancas, one of the most popular tourist attractions on the navy base, and the Sherman Cove Marina with its dozens of water craft.

For a quarter of a mile, the PARCOURSE meanders along an old, two-lane, asphalt highway which was traveled in bygone days but has become a relic of the past. The segment of the trail that passes Sherman Field can be extremely noisy when the training aircraft are taking off and landing. For the most part, however, the PARCOURSE is a secluded walk. One section runs through the deep, silent woods. One summer morning I was walking this portion of the trail when a fox ran across my path. The animal darted from the tangle of pines and palmettos, paused long enough on the trail to stare me in the eye, then disappeared into the forest. This morning I spy no fox. Only a few lizards and a rat cross the shadow of my footfalls. The most comforting section of the PARCOURSE for me is the stretch approaching the old lighthouse. Here the underbrush grows dense, the oaks strong and massive, and the footpath is littered with straw and fallen leaves. The historic black and white lighthouse in the clearing stands as a towering monument to days gone by, when sailors in their eagerness to make port forgot about the dangerous shallow waters. Something about the ancient beacon appeals to me. I pause in the shade of a spreading oak and contemplate the concrete monolith. What is there about this antiquated lighthouse that whispers so alluringly to my soul? Is it the light in the tower that beckons the lonely seaman home? I yearn for home. I am a wandering pilgrim longing for my eternal home. I am a restless soul lost in the maelstrom of life, searching for the shore on the other side, watching and hoping for the Light of the World who guides me. Strange, how an old beacon conjures up the most intimate yearnings of my soul.

A hundred yards beyond Lighthouse Point stands a live oak tree. This giant oak, with its massive trunk and overarching limbs, is the most beautiful tree my civilization-blinded eyes have seen. Its symmetry could not be more perfect had an artist's hand painted it on a piece of canvas. It is the consummate tree. As I stand before the tree engulfed in wonder, I recognize the touch of the Artist who painted the universe. Eventually my journey leads me beyond the quiet woods. I find myself traversing a sandy path that twists and turns along the water's edge. The Gulf of Mexico is calm this morning. The water is smooth and blue with golden sunlight glinting off the surface like sparkling diamonds. The terrain is scrub brush and palmetto bushes. Beyond the palmettos, I approach a marshy area of swaying cattails growing out of brackish water. The yellow sign mounted against the wooden footbridge warns pedestrians to "Beware of the Alligator." Obviously, a gator calls this little space of marsh home (although I never see him). The cautious part of my personality peels a wary eye. The adventuresome part of me, too long hidden, tells me to take off my shoes and wade into the swampy lagoon. I fear I am becoming too civilized in my middle years. The fountain at the trail's turnaround point yields no drinking water this morning. Someone turned off the fountain at its source. Going without the thirst-quenching, life-renewing elixir is no problem for me, for I have learned how to survive on scarcity. I retrace my steps to the beginning of the course where old people stroll and young sailors jog and where automobiles wait silently in the parking lot. I have found the peace for which my soul came searching.

# Walking to
# Serenity Beach

*I suggest that we experience times of
fasting from people, not because we
are antisocial, but precisely because
we love people intensely and when we
are with them we want to be able to
do them good....*

— Richard J. Foster

You won't find Serenity Beach on a map or tourist
brochure. There is no stretch of shoreline officially
named Serenity Beach. Yet the water on Serenity Beach
runs as blue, the sand sparkles as sugar white, and
the horizon looms as vast and endless as any seashore

---

tourist trap marked on a visitor's guide. I dubbed this remote stretch of sand and water Serenity Beach because of the soothing effect it has on my soul. On calm days the only sounds that reach the ear are the lonely cries of sea gulls in flight and the easy lapping of the surf as it licks a soggy shore. On rough days the gulf pommels the helpless coastline with ruthless vengeance. Foamy white waves rise and curl five feet above the greenish-black depths. Serenity Beach has many moods; each speaks comfort to my beleaguered spirit.

There are two avenues of access to Serenity Beach. You drive to the end of the road, where the broken blacktop gives way to loose gravel and crushed shells. You exit the highway at its terminus and cautiously steer your way along the crunching truck path until it wanders into a one-lane trail with sea oats sprouting between seldom-used ruts. When the primitive tracks run out, you know you have reached Serenity Beach. You climb the rolling dunes and gaze across the undisturbed water and deserted coastline. The other way, if you can free yourself from the appointment calendar and time clock, and don't mind a strenuous hike through sand, is to stuff a towel and a couple of liters of water into a backpack and walk to it. An hour of walking along the shoreline takes you beyond the public beach with its crowded pavilions, swimmers, and sun worshipers. Today my soul requires the silence and solitude Serenity Beach offers. I must spend a few hours off the beaten path— away from a ringing telephone, away from a desk piled with books and papers, away from the demands my vocation makes on me.

The hour is early when I park my truck in the public access area. Since the journey is as important as the destination, I choose to walk to Serenity Beach on this cool, windswept morning while black thunderheads roll in from the horizon. The blustery weather conjures up a feeling of loneliness within me. I feel overwhelmed by the frightening sensation that I am the only person in the world, a solitary figure drinking in the breathtaking spectacle of creation. I fight the impulse to turn around and run back to the confusion, familiarity and safety of civilization. The solitary trek along the deserted beach gives me the space I need to plumb the depths of my soul. My ruminations unearth a multitude of emotions. I pause to bury a pile of empty beer cans, their telling stench the last remnants of lost souls who exist on the periphery of life. I struggle to make sense of these modern Epicureans who eat, drink, and make merry, who do not understand that tomorrow they die. I am confused by those persons who pass through this world without seeing or feeling the beauty around them, who litter time and space with the refuse of their drunken orgies. A blue heron spreads its majestic wings in panic-stricken flight as my footfalls approach. A gaggle of gulls dances across the packed sand snatching sand crabs too slow to reach the safety of the burrows they dug into the grass-matted dunes. "Fear not, little flock, for it is your Father's good pleasure to give you the kingdom" (Luke 12:32).

A hundred yards ahead I catch sight of a kite trapped in the swirling air currents. I watch the pink and purple triangle as it soars, dives, and circles, at times coming within a few feet of the ground but never crashing. The silence is broken by the thunderous roar of a squadron of fighter jets screaming through the air in pyramid formation. Their mighty engines ravage the fragile tranquility for which my heart desperately searches. The planes disappear into the angry sky just as quickly as they came, a trail of white vapor the only evidence they passed this way. My thoughts return to the silent landscape around me. The decaying carcass of a blue crab litters the beach. Its button-like eyes stare in a fixed trance across the tumultuous waters, as if the animal died longing for its homeland. I sense the desperation this tiny sea creature must have felt the brief spark that was its life flickered and died. I understand the yearning in its heart for a home. This world of time and space and people is not my home. I am a pilgrim on the earth, a stranger, a sojourner passing through. My heart is set on a better place—a place where death and pain and misery are no more; a place where there will be no more grief, no more heartache, "for the former things have passed away" (Rev. 21:4).

The attractions and noises of the public world slowly recede into the background—out of sight, out of mind, out of heart and soul. The solitude of the deserted shoreline wraps itself around me like a comfortable blanket. The stiff wind that stirs the gulf lashes my shirt. My body begins to shiver. A clear image of the blue windbreaker I left behind takes shape in my imagination. A piece of driftwood the size of a tree trunk invites me to pause and gaze across the infinite horizon. I am drawn into a moment of meditation before the advancing autumn weather drives me on. At last I reach Serenity Beach. Here I find silence, solitude, and peace. Here I experience a few precious hours away from my busy lifestyle. Here I do not have to do anything; I can sit still and reflect and be touched by feelings. A rainbow of color unfolds before my eyes. Serenity Beach is awash with tiny seashells—red, gray, yellow, pink, and mauve. I lose myself in the beauty of the moment as a loving God hides me in the vast, eternal silence.

# Strolling the Road
# from Melrose

*There was such a repose and quiet
here at this hour, as if the very hillsides were enjoying the scene, and we
passed slowly along, looking back
over the country we had traversed....*
— Henry David Thoreau

Ella and I are part of a tour group visiting England
and Scotland. We are aboard a motor coach traveling
across the entrancing Scottish countryside. Scotland
is an enchanting country, astonishing in its beauty.
Picturesque fishing villages line the craggy shores of
the North Sea and the North Atlantic Ocean. Quaint

hamlets of gray stone edifices punctuate the land-scape. From the hidden depths of Loch Lomond to the balding summits of the Highlands, Scotland is a land of austere contrasts. Seventy percent of its five million people live in Aberdeen, Edinburgh, Glasgow, and other urban areas. But the country is most noted for its rugged mountains, green valleys, and bottom-less blue lakes. Around ten o'clock on this bright July morning our bus rolls into the tiny village of Melrose. Melrose is so small I have difficulty locating it in the atlas. The town's only claim to fame is that it was the home of Elizabeth Cecelia Clephane, the poet who wrote the well-known Christian hymn, "Beneath the Cross of Jesus." Elizabeth Clephane was born in Melrose in 1830, and died there in 1869. The towns-people called her the Sunbeam of Melrose. She spent most of her life doing charitable deeds for people in need. Elizabeth Clephane wrote poetry when she was not helping neighbors or strangers. She penned the lines of the hymn in the summer of 1868, after study-ing the life and ministry of Augustus Toplady, the writer of "Rock of Ages." Elizabeth Clephane remains Melrose's most famous citizen more than a century after her death. Melrose's only tourist attractions are its numerous woolen shops where travelers can buy sweaters, scarves, and other garments made from Scotland's notable sheep industry.

The ruins of a twelfth century Cistercian monas-tery litter the outskirts of town. English invaders destroyed the monastery hundreds of years ago, but some of the abbey's massive columns and sacred arches still stand in silent tribute to the simple life of prayer, fasting, and labor the brown-robed monks led. A narrow country lane winds its way through the storybook village of Melrose. The pathway tugs ever so gently at my heartstrings. I observed the rolling acres and flowing streams from behind the glass windows of our coach; while we are stopped in Melrose I must lose myself in the beauty of my surroundings. I leave our excited group of sightseers to spend their pounds in the woolen shops and perhaps take on a few extra pounds in the pastry shops. With a warm sun against my face and a quiet joy in my heart, I strike out along the twisting trail. I feel comforted, nestled between the dense hedgerows that line the highway. Before me lie rich green pastures, tall with grain, some sprinkled with grazing sheep. Over my right shoulder stand the three hills of Sir Walter Scott. The hills call to me in a whispered but inviting voice. I regret my time here is too short to explore them. The road from Melrose takes me past a field of knee-high grass a farmer plans to cut for hay. In one pasture which has been cut, a horseshoe-shaped stand of hay bales waits to be thrown to hungry cattle and sheep when the weather turns cold. I find myself drawn to this secluded hiding place. I step off the road and enter the unseen silence waiting within the hay's walls. I seize the moment of seclusion to fantasize that I alone exist. Someday I hope to lose myself in the vast, hidden silence of God.

As I continue my journey along the nearly-deserted highway, an inner voice shouts, "What a glorious morning for a walk!" The air feels crisp. A yolk-like sun plays hide-and-seek behind piles of billowing clouds. I feel the pulse of the day throbbing in my spirit. The word saunter plays across the fields of my mind. Saunter comes from the time-worn words sacred and terra; it means to walk in a sacred manner. Saunter is the term the crusaders used to describe their pilgrimages to the Holy Land. My stroll from Melrose becomes a pilgrimage, and the world around me is a shrine. One day I hope to saunter along a country lane that winds to no place special; I hope to travel a road that has no end, that keeps twisting and turning into infinity. A yellow construction truck parked along the roadside reminds me I am still part of the world of time and space. Two workmen spend their morning break eating sandwiches and gulping soft drinks in the vehicle's cab. As I stroll past the two laborers, I wonder if their fatigue prevents them from seeing the glory of the moment as much as my work days exhaust and blind me to the beauty of God's creation. A twenty-minute walk brings me to the town of Newstead, a little more than a mile from Melrose. A brownstone bridge marks the city limits. Attracted to this quaint little community off the beaten path, I would like to linger and visit, but a quick check of my watch tells me our tour bus will pull out of Melrose in thirty minutes. My journey ends on the brown rock bridge overlooking a bubbling creek on the outskirts of Newstead. I retrace my steps to Melrose, gazing again at the fallen trees and grassy fields that separate the two picturesque villages. I will not pass this way again, but my soul has found its home.

# Remembering a
# Covered Bridge

*What to do with this inner wound
that is so easily touched and starts
bleeding again? It is such a familiar
wound. It has been with me for many
years.*

— Henri Nouwen

The wonderful time machine called memory takes me back more years than I care to count. I become ten years old again, a curious child filled with awe, alive to the sights and sounds of my innocent world. I see the old homestead where I romped during carefree summers. Uncle Vernon owned the property, but the place belonged to all of us who savored the fresh scent of grass after a summer rain, who were thrilled with the beauty of wild cherry blossoms, and who enjoyed the ooze of wet mud between our toes. In my mind's eye I see the vintage farmhouse crowning the hillside like an emerald tiara adorning a queen, its wooden sides stained with paint as green as a mountain meadow. I remember the aging cabin's freshly waxed floors, its massive gray stone fireplace littered with ash, and the extended oak kitchen table flanked on both sides with backless benches. I hear the rain softly splattering against the tin roof, and I recall how its rhythmic pitter-patter lulled us children to sleep during long, lazy afternoons. The elongated front porch that ran from one corner of the house to the other comes to mind. I recollect sitting in the handmade cane chairs aligned in a row along the porch's edge and propping my feet on the sapling rail that had been sanded smooth from years of gentle stroking. I envision the friendly haven this open sanctuary offered on summer evenings. I remember those I loved— Uncle Vernon, Aunt Ludie, Mama and Daddy, cousins, and playmates—sitting on the porch and talking at the end of the day. Most of the people here I loved have died or moved on to other places in their lives; but their easy laughter and the soft hum of their conversation still rings in my ears. From my vantage on the front porch, I gaze longingly across the yard, beyond the blooming pink and red camellia bushes, beyond the yellow honeysuckle lacing the barbed wire fence. My eyes come to rest on the creosote-stained gate, sagging with years of swinging to and fro. I hear the squeaking rusty hinges and the cows lowing in the pasture beyond. I glimpse the dilapidated hay barn in the far corner of the pasture and the stand of massive oaks that offered cooling shade beneath a blistering Georgia sun.

A hard-packed clay road curved its way eastward from the old homestead. The road twisted and turned among a mosaic of birch, pine, maple, and pecan groves. In my memory I find myself walking the country lane again. I feel its concrete-like dirt beneath my bare feet. I take note of the tiny white pebbles that glinted in the sun at the road's edge. My throat parches in the thick swirl of dust stirred up by the dry summer breeze. Once again I am lost in the simple grandeur of this antiquated world of plum trees and blackberry bushes. I recall the historic covered bridge which spanned the creek that flowed through the gorge, interrupting the lane's meandering journey. I have a vivid memory of the bridge's sturdy timbers and the massive iron stakes that held it immovable against countless processions of horses, wagons, and automobiles. I still hear the hollow-sounding echoes of excited children running from one end of its wooden archway to the other. I am one of those children, barefooted and without a shirt, asking nothing more from life than an afternoon of pleasure. As I playfully skip across the old bridge, I glance down between its crossties at the bubbling creek rushing underneath. I recall swimming in the creek's cool, untainted waters. The creek was a special swimming hole for us children. We cleared away the rocks and debris, the thickets and briars. We chased away the moccasins and copperheads and claimed this spot as our domain. The swimming hole was our refuge from the world of chores and responsibilities and adults. I feel again the splash of its sparkling flow against my face. I hear once more the excited whoops of childhood playmates as we swing from vines and swear allegiance forever.

Sometimes I long to go back to the old farmhouse. I long to sit on its front porch and prop my feet on the sapling rail. I long to eat another meal at its family table and sleep under its tin roof on a rainy night. I need to run across the cow pasture, smell the honeysuckle, and hide from imaginary enemies in the hay barn. I yearn to saunter along the red clay road and pick the rich harvest of berries that grow alongside. I hunger for the sweet taste of wild blackberries on my tongue. I want to frolic in the hollow of the old covered bridge, listen to the echoes of children's shouts, and swim in the river with my friends. I need those lazy summer days of innocence, hope, and happiness, but those days are gone forever. The Corps of Engineers bought the land where the old homestead stood. They tore down the house and demolished the covered bridge. They submerged the pastures and woodlands under a recreational lake. Uncle Vernon died. Aunt Ludie died. Dad died. Mom grows older. I lost touch with my cousins and playmates years ago. The years move in steady progression. Times and people change. As I recall bittersweet memories from the perspective of four decades later, I find comfort in the knowledge that there is One who never changes. "Jesus Christ is the same yesterday and today and forever" (Heb. 13:8). Life moves on like a river flowing beneath a covered bridge; but the constant, unchanging love of Jesus protects and sustains us at every turn.

# Sightseeing in Provincetown

*Life is more than a task to be performed.*
— Frank W. Gunsaulus

Provincetown, Massachusetts lies at the extreme tip of Cape Cod. Vacationers who seek to experience the town's unique personality must traverse an isolated countryside of sand dunes and scrub brush. When they come to the place where the highway meets the rugged Atlantic Ocean, they reach Provincetown. Many tourists travel to Provincetown to capture a moment of history. Provincetown Harbor is the spot where the Pilgrims dropped anchor when they came to America. The little band of English Separatists came ashore where Provincetown now stands on November 21, 1620; but they did not stay long on the jagged strip of coastline. Recognizing their need for a better harbor, they used Provincetown as a temporary refuge while they scouted the area for a permanent settlement. The Pilgrims eventually chose Plymouth as the site for their colony; but the citizens of Provincetown and the state of Massachusetts acknowledge the role the remote region played in the colonization of America. A monument commemorating the signing of the Mayflower Compact stands near the center of Provincetown, and a park at the edge of town marks the spot where the Pilgrims first set foot in the new world.

Over the years Provincetown seems to have earned a reputation as a protected harbor for individuals and groups seeking the liberty to live by their own codes, free from the oppression of society and unencumbered by traditional mores. Today's community is not your typical American hamlet where the Stars and Stripes unfurl from every window and where middle-class men and women espouse orthodox values. Provincetown is a counter-culture colony where those who do not fit the mold of society thrive. Artists, poets, musicians, and others who march to the beat of their own drum congregate in Provincetown because the enclave provides them a safe place to express their eccentric lifestyles without fear of rejection or reprisal. Main Street is lined with wine and cheese shops, espresso cafes, and book nooks. You will not find a K-Mart or a Wal-Mart in Provincetown. The eight-thousand permanent residents of Provincetown live on the margin of America, not only in a geographical and cultural sense, but also from an economic perspective. The community depends heavily on the tourist industry to keep it financially afloat. Shop owners must bring in the major portion of their incomes between April and October. If they don't make money during the tourist season, they don't make it at all. Many small businesses don't survive the lean, cold winter months. Others barely scrape by. The average annual income of the citizens of Provincetown is $30,000—the lowest annual income of any city in Massachusetts.

The late poet Harry Kemp exemplifies the Bohemian spirit of Provincetown. Kemp came to Provincetown in 1916 to perform in Eugene O'Neill's first play, *Bound East for Cardiff,* and died there 43 years later. Kemp became known to the residents of Provincetown as the Poet of the Dunes. He lived without indoor plumbing in one of the infamous "dune shacks" hidden among the gigantic sand dunes that tower over the ocean's edge. Kemp wrote about the silent beauty of the moon shimmering on the water. He wrote about the sea breezes of summer and the chilling winds of winter. He also described how it felt to live in a shack made of rotting timber with no toilet and a roof that leaks. Kemp was the champion of the unencumbered life.

I find myself drawn to Provincetown on a peaceful afternoon when summer lies before me like a lazy lover dozing in the sunshine. I am attracted to the quaint village not because of the role the area played in the founding of our country, but because of the unique identity the community has carved out for itself in contemporary society. At the age of fifty, when I anticipated my life would be settling into a comfortable pattern of predictability, I discover myself embarking on an unfamiliar pilgrimage; and Provincetown, with its different cadence, becomes one of the holy places I must visit. One morning, several years ago, I crawled out of bed looked in the bathroom mirror and did not recognize the individual who returned my gaze. My ink black beard had faded to gray. Puffy, dark circles had taken up residence underneath my eyes. The waistline that had remained trim over the decades hung in a bundle of drooping skin. I was growing older. In spite of the healthy regimen of long distance running I had practiced for 20 years, I was losing the battle of advancing age. The emotional changes that took place within me at mid-life were as compelling, if not as noticeable, as the physical changes. During a prolonged period of self-examination, I faced the frightening truth that I was not happy with the way my life had turned out. My two sons, around whom my younger years had revolved, stood on the threshold of adulthood and no longer needed me in the ways they once had. My wife of nearly three decades was blossoming into her own person with a fulfilling career and professional relationships that did not include me. Even the call to ministry, which had been so exhilarating and challenging, was becoming little more than a routine job to be tolerated.

When I reflected on the cherished hopes and dreams of my early adulthood, I felt dismayed to discover how few of those visions I had been able to transform into reality. The foundations on which I had built my existence were shifting. I was reaching a transition point in my life which confronted me with two choices. I could continue living the way I had lived for so many years, even though the lifestyle no longer fulfilled me; or I could begin to make some changes in the way I lived. Despite the gnawing sense of restlessness that ate away at my insides like a slow-growing cancer, turning my back and walking away from 30 years of marriage and ministry was never an option for me as I confronted my mid-life problems. I was not the kind of person to throw up my hands in desperation and run away. In my work as a pastor I had counseled too many men and women who had walked away from their families and careers only to regret their decision later. So I decided to adjust my lifestyle within the family and vocational boundaries I had chosen.

I modified the unrealistic career ambitions I had harbored for a quarter of a century. I stepped off the ecclesiastical ladder of success and became content with the medium-sized congregation I served and the average salary I earned. I peeled off the coat and necktie I often wore and substituted denim jeans and pullover shirts. I let my hair grow to shoulder length and began spending several afternoons each week in a coffeehouse where I wrote poems and essays and kept a journal. I published a volume of poetry which described the lost opportunities of my youth and the vanishing career ambitions of my future. The pilgrimage through the middle years was not as much a journey of re-creating myself as it was a process of uncovering the authentic self buried beneath layers of social, religious, family, and career expectations. This is why Provincetown, with its different drumbeat, is a holy place for me. At mid-life I heard the unique cadence of my drum and I sought for the courage to march to it.

I realize I never will break free completely from the chains of conventionalism. I am too much a product of orthodoxy to embrace wholeheartedly the Bohemian lifestyle of Harry Kemp. I am too accustomed to middle-class comforts to exist on the fringe of society in a dune shack without indoor plumbing. But I cherish that aspect of my personality that steers me in a different direction from the herd of humanity. The eccentric element of my personality takes me beyond purposeful existence to meaningful living. It allows me to experience a dimension of satisfaction I previously did not know existed. Perhaps I finally am discovering the quality of life to which Jesus referred when he said, "I came that they may have life, and have it abundantly" (John 10:10).

On a leisurely afternoon when summer beckoned, I strolled along the streets of Provincetown, a quaint village off the beaten path, and considered the new direction my life was taking. There is more to see in Provincetown than meets the eye.

# PART 3

# *Altars*

# Climbing an
# Austrian Alp

*Great things are done when men and*
*mountains meet; this is not done by*
*jostling in the street.*

— William Blake

Silence takes many forms. It comes as the mere
absence of noise when the television waits quietly in
the corner of the room or when the traffic subsides
on the busy highway. Silence appears as an inner
stillness when the heart remains calm despite the
jostle of the crowd. There is the silence that comes
with solitude, the silence of walking alone through
the deep woods while listening to an autumn
wind rattle brittle leaves. Every silence pales in

---

comparison to the ultimate silence found while standing atop a 10,000-foot mountain. Our tour group lodges in the quaint ski village of Ischgl, Austria, in the heart of Alpine country. The majestic, snow-covered Alps have been singing their love song to me since the moment our party arrived. And so, on a morning when most of the people in our group travel to Oberammergau to watch the celebrated passion play, I give my soul to the mountains. Today will be my only opportunity to immerse myself in their grandeur and disappear into their mystery.

The cool summer morning finds me hiking a narrow dirt logging road that snakes up the side of one of the towering peaks. The angle of ascent is so steep I must lean forward to compensate. The calves in my legs tighten, and my lungs burn as I drag myself steadily up the twisting, turning roadway. Pulling myself up this grade helps me understand why trail hikers carry walking sticks; they need the poles not to frighten away predators which might stalk their steps, but as leverage when walking uphill. After 30 minutes of climbing, I ascend to the underbelly of the clouds which hang heavy and gray across the Austrian sky. The hotels and restaurants of Ischgl in the valley look like buildings from a child's toy village. During a rest stop, my gaze falls on a red-tipped road marker pointing up the side of the mountain. The arrow-like marker points toward a red blaze on a massive oak. I have stumbled onto a hunting trail. Digging my fingers and toes into the wall of dirt that forms the inside edge of the roadway, I leave the road and strike out straight up the side of the mountain, the red blazes my only guides. I pick my way through ankle-deep mud beneath tree limbs so dense they block the morning sun. At last I emerge from the shady thickets into a warm, sun-drenched meadow where clumps of daisies smile from grassy knolls. I rest on a wooden bridge and dangle my feet in the icy stream that cascades from the melting snow above. I contemplate what it means to live halfway between earth and heaven. Earth is a twilight world of half-reality where I seek God and hide from God in the same motion. Yet here in this lonely realm of snow-covered peaks, I experience no ambivalence. Here my only desire is to lose myself in the presence of God. I must leave the man-made world of buildings, people, and confusion and enter a universe of silence. I must gaze upon "a building from God, a house not made with hands, eternal in the heavens" (II Cor. 5:1). I must know this bald, fresh domain of the spirit; I must scale its most distant rock and stand with raised arms on its loftiest, loneliest peak.

The oaks and evergreens give way to scrub brush beyond the timberline. The brush surrenders to rocks and patches of grass sprinkled with Edelweiss and wild mountain roses. The clouds linger timidly below, as if sensing their unworthiness to ascend into this snow-covered holy place. A cold wind blows eternally new upon this ancient, silent monolith. Three hours have passed since I left the world below, my world of confusion. Such a brief moment separating time from eternity, existence from abundant life.

At last I stand atop the summit of this majestic Alp; I enter the Holy of Holies, the great divide between heaven and earth. The world I know—the world of noise, stress, and anxiety—lies below, hidden from sight for the time being. The world I long to know— a domain of silence, spirit, and contemplation— awaits at my outstretched fingertips. The breeze that swirls around my shoulders is the divine breath drawing me upward to my eternal home. The world of time and space lies littered with holy places—churches, temples, synagogues, mosques—shrines and altars to a myriad of superfluous gods. Only one God haunts the solitude of this holy mountain. Only the Living God fills the emptiness of this eternal moment.

The Gospel of Luke tells of Jesus climbing the Mount of Transfiguration with Peter, James and John. On the summit of the mountain, Jesus spoke with Moses and Elijah about the impending crucifixion and resurrection. Peter was so overcome with awe that he suggested the group take up residence on the mountain: And as the men were parting from him, Peter said to Jesus, "Master, it is well that we are here; let us make three booths, one for you and one for Moses and one for Elijah"—not knowing what he said (Luke 9:33).

Standing on the summit of this ten-thousand-foot Austrian Alp, surrounded by ice and snow and holy silence, I comprehend the depth of Peter's passion.

On the mountain we find more than stillness; we find utter stillness. On the mountain we discover more than silence; we discover complete silence. On the mountain we experience solitude beyond aloneness. We come into the holy presence of the eternal God. We meet the same God Moses met in the mystery of Sinai, the same Father to whom Jesus prayed in the hills of Galilee, the same Provider and Sustainer the prophet Elijah encountered in the safety of Horeb.

I run and play in the snow like a child. I stand in silence and watch and listen. I look to heaven in awe and wonder. I bow my knee and open my heart in adoration. I am alone with God. I am the creature romping in the Creator's playground under God's loving, watchful care. I am the weary pilgrim who has reached the end of his journey. Before the daylight vanishes into the approaching darkness I will return to the world below. We cannot remain on the mountain forever—not Peter nor James nor John, and certainly not I. Our lives must be lived in the valley of human need. Here, on the holy mountain, my soul shall dwell forever.

# Crossing Loch Lomond

*We travel in silence.*

— St. John of the Cross

A grizzled sailor stands on the wooden dock flashing a snaggletoothed grin. I press a five pound note into his hand and brush past his shoulder toward the gangplank of the old steamer which ferries tourists back and forth across Loch Lomond. A narrow, iron walkway guides me onto the ship's lower deck. In an attempt to secure a better view of the glory that will unfold around me, I climb the steep, winding stairway that leads to the upper deck. I rest my forearms against the red metal rail that encloses the open-air area and wait for my fellow passengers to board. The vast expanse of cloudless blue sky feels liberating in contrast to the morning coach ride. The cold Scottish summer breeze awakens me from the sluggish stupor into which I drifted during the crowded bus ride.

Loch Lomond is Scotland's largest lake. Tucked away in one of the country's remote valleys, the fresh water loch runs twenty-three miles north and south; it spans five miles across at its widest point. Loch Lomond needs no mystical sea monster (like the Loch Ness) to capture my fascination. I am spellbound by its black, hidden depths that wait out of sight beneath my feet. My heart pounds with anticipation as I ponder the thought of sailing across its murky, silent waters.

After our party of thirty has boarded safely, the captain pulls up the gangplank and fastens the access gate. The ship's engine roars to life; its cannon-like bellow shatters the stilled sanctity of the moment. The helmsman nudges the throttle forward. Our travel brochure bills the excursion as a one-hour cruise on Scotland's most beautiful lake. To me the adventure transcends physical boundaries; this is a journey into my soul, a fantasy cruise into a world of wonder, joy, and exaltation. I feel transported beyond humanity's minuscule, finite realm of sight.

The ship slowly cuts through the lake's tranquil waters. The purr of the motor at cruising speed acts as a sedative on my agitated existence. I stand on the port bow, feeling the wind in my face, and gaze at the massive granite mountains rising out of Loch Lomond's bottomless bowels. The shoreline lies blanketed with long-leafed pine, cedar, and blue spruce. Our ship's mate tells us about a hiking trail that cuts through the dense wooded area encircling the lake. Her voice fades from my hearing as I retreat into my private domain of daydreams. I envision myself with a pack strapped to my back, plotting my course along the winding footpath.

We have navigated only three miles of Loch Lomond's opaque depths when we round a bend and come upon a company of children playing on boulders at the lake's edge. Some of the children are scrambling from rock to rock; others are splashing in the chilling waters, like sea creatures at play. I am captivated by how unconstrained the youngsters appear, and I wonder what it feels like to be free from the sense of mission, to be released from the awful burden of responsibility that consumes me.

Nearby, a waterfall, clear and pristine in its descent, splashes over boulders from its source high in the mountains and washes into the placid lake waters. "Somewhere there is a hidden, secret fountain that replenishes our lives," I whisper to myself. I recall the words Jesus spoke at the feast of Tabernacles: "If any one thirst, let him come to me and drink. He who believes in me, as the scripture has said, 'Out of his heart shall flow rivers of living water'" (John 7:37-38). A commotion above my head snaps me back to reality. A flock of sea gulls has descended upon our boat. As many as two dozen birds trail our wake—climbing, diving, circling in majestic loops. Someone tosses a broken soda cracker into the air. An alert gull snatches the morsel with its beak and veers off like a fighter pilot fleeing harm's way. Soon all 30 people in our party are tossing cookie crumbs toward the heavens. One of the graceful white creatures flies to within three feet of my outstretched arm. I open my palm and flip a sugar cube left over from my tea. The bird snares the tiny square with its scissors-like bill. As soon as the gull samples the cube's syrupy sweet taste, its beak opens and lets the lump fall into the bottomless waters.

Jesus counseled his followers, "Look at the birds of the air" (Mt. 5:26). The gull's refusal of my tainted offering calls to mind how consumed humanity has become with things that do not satisfy. We humans gorge ourselves on the empty, the shallow, the sensational—on contrivances which have no substance. In spite of our intelligence, we reject the lesson a simple bird in flight understands—how to purse our lips and spew a toxic world from our mouths. In spite of our knowledge and technological advances, we remain a culture without wisdom. We are blinded by our neon cities. We are melted by our hot, lustful passions.

The hour on Loch Lomond passes quickly. The dock comes in view around an elbow of trees and shrubs. The megaphone on the ship's stern crackles as the captain relays instructions on disembarking. In a handful of minutes I will find myself back inside a cramped tour bus, looking wistfully at the world through glass windows. At the moment, however, inspiration pulses through my being and rapture fills my soul.

# Strolling through an Apple Orchard

*I fear that he who walks over these fields a century hence will not know the pleasure of knocking off wild apples.*

— Henry David Thoreau

Our youngest son Matthew worked on the staff of Fort Bluff Camp for two summers. Fort Bluff is an Independent Baptist camp owned by Mike and Naomi Crane. Fort Bluff sits on a mountain overlooking the sleepy town of Dayton, Tennessee. Mike Crane holds a black belt in Tae Kwon Do and Naomi possesses one of the loveliest singing voices I have ever heard. Few places rival Fort Bluff when it comes to inspiring a sense of awe. The camp's log cabins are rustic. The dirt and gravel road circling the compound is lined on both sides with an aging wooden fence. The acres of grass are immaculately cropped. The landscape is sprinkled with rock-bordered flower gardens. A freshly painted walking bridge gently arcs across a pond so placid one can catch one's unbroken reflection in the waters. Goldfish the size of bream swim in the pond's tranquil depths, while ducks and geese strut around its edges.

For many visitors the camp's most inspirational point is the bluff—a rocky ledge jutting out over the edge of Mike's mountain. From the bluff one can gaze across the panoramic grandeur of hundreds of miles of Tennessee forests, watch the Tennessee River as it slowly meanders across the state, and spot cattle so remote they look like ants crawling on the pasture's green carpet of grass. The bluff is a sacred place, especially when dawn breaks over the cool stillness of night, offering a clean, fresh beginning to the new day. My visit to Fort Bluff this summer reveals a shrine equally as inspirational as the view from the mountain, a holy place I did not notice when I came here last summer. Across the graveled, rutted lane from the cubby-hole room where Ella and I are staying stands an apple orchard. The orchard consists of a half-dozen apple trees growing on a grassy knoll. Two of the trees stand empty except for the limbs full of bushy leaves. A third tree bears a handful of small, greenish-red apples scattered throughout its branches.

The other trees hang rich and full with red, ripe fruit the size of tennis balls. When I discover these living, towering monuments, their sturdy limbs bending to the ground beneath the weight of apples, I can do nothing except stand in silence and adore the God who understood my silly request to see an apple tree.

Several months ago I came across Henry David Thoreau's essay on wild apples. Thoreau wrote of the delicious fruit with a passion which kindled in me the desire to saunter through an apple orchard and handle the crop on the trees. I wanted to clutch a piece of the firm, red fruit in my hand and taste its tangy flavor on the back of my tongue. When Thoreau predicted there would be no more wild apples one day, I began to consider how many years I had gone without seeing an apple tree laden with fruit. I could not remember the last time I walked leisurely through a field thick with apple trees.

Consequently, as I stroll through Naomi's apple orchard on this August morning, looking with reverence at the bushy, green leaves and rubescent pieces of fruit, I recognize more than picture-book trees and delicious apples. I realize that I am walking across hallowed ground. I hear the divine voice Moses heard as the prophet approached the burning bush: "Put off your shoes from your feet, for the place on which you are standing is holy ground" (Ex. 3:5). As I stand in the midst of the apple trees, taking in their beauty, I discern God's answer to my prayers to see an apple orchard. God satisfies the hunger of my soul. The Lord who fed the children of Israel with manna in the wilderness also fulfills my needs.

There don't seem to be many apple orchards in this day and age. Sadly, Thoreau's prophecy is coming true. Our clutching and clamoring society finds things to do with its land other than grow apple trees on it. No landowner with an eye for business would plant an apple orchard on a vacant lot when he could erect a shopping center on the property and lease it for a million dollars. Why plant a half-dozen trees when corporate-owned farms grow and ship the fruit by the truckload? Most of us buy our apples in the supermarket anyway.

The modern world knows little about apples, huckleberries, acorns, and other such sacred objects. To me, these simple items reflect the grace of God.

# Camping in
# the Deep Woods

*To deliver oneself up, to hand oneself
over, to entrust oneself completely to
the silence of a wide landscape of
woods.... This is a true and special
vocation.*

— Thomas Merton

My home tonight is simple. The packed dirt beneath
my feet serves as a floor. Heaven is my ceiling. The
scattered trees and shrubs become walls. My chair is
a toppled oak; the fireplace and kitchen, a circle of
stones. I feel content surrounded by these basic
elements of life. Why should anyone require more?

The day was unusually hot and humid for this
time of year. The journey proved long and exhausting. I said my goodbyes to civilization around one
o'clock in the afternoon. With the barest of necessi-
ties—food, water, and a change of clothing—strapped

against my back, I pushed my way into the expansive forest. One compulsion drove each step: I felt the necessity of spending a few uninterrupted moments alone with God. I needed to hear the still, small voice whisper in my ear. I wanted to feel the touch of God's gentle hand upon my shoulder.

At the outset of the journey, the clamor of a busy world pierced my ears and intruded into my thoughts. I heard the whine of automobiles on a nearby highway. The dull drone of an airplane broke over my head. My soul felt the clutter of appointments and schedules, of meaningless conversations and unending requests. The deeper into the vast wilderness I tramped, the dimmer the distractions grew and the more placid the pool of peace within my heart became. By the end of the day I had entered a sphere untainted by the destructive hand of progress. I found myself alone in creation as God fashioned it—raw, pristine, and fresh; a world without sound, without time, without movement except that of my intrusion.

Now as the daylight hours fade with a hush behind rolling hills, I sit staring into the flickering orange of my campfire, its flames licking into a black sky. In the shadows I glimpse twisted tree limbs still naked from the onslaught of winter. A benevolent Creator soon will clothe the world with the greenery of spring. I glance at the plebeian mountain tent staked in a stand of sweet gum trees. Its open flap calls to my aging bones and weary muscles, but I will not succumb to its seduction—at least not yet. Overhead a sprinkling of stars shimmers against a black velvet background. In the distance I detect the faint glow of another campfire. Somewhere on a lonely hillside a few miles away another seeker waits before his own flicker of hope, his heart pounding with the same wonder that now pulses in my breast.

I crouch against my fallen oak chair and slowly rotate a sharpened stick over the open flame. The meal of bread and meat is like the life for which I hunger— simple, basic, solid and without pretense. I am mesmerized by the licking fire and lost in a private world of thought.

We humans make our existences too complicated. We build elaborate homes to gratify our egos rather than meet our needs. We waste our meager incomes on overpriced cars and trucks so we can drive around the block. We stumble out of bed each morning to the screeching of electronic alarms. We rush to cubicle offices where we spend our days quarreling with colleagues and computers. Our heads pound and our hearts fail. Our fast-paced, clutching lifestyles blind us to God's simple offer of grace. Our incessant striving deafens us to the voice of Christ: "Let not your hearts be troubled; believe in God, believe also in me" (Jn. 14:1). "Peace I leave with you; my peace I give to you. I do not give to you as the world gives. Do not let your hearts be troubled, and do not let them be afraid" (Jn. 14:27).

Spending these hours in the solitude of the deep woods and hearing the divine voice as it whistles through the winter trees helps me to put my exist- ence into perspective. I am a child of God, saved by grace, and living each day under the watchful care of my heavenly Father. There is no need for me to feel anxious and fretful; God will provide everything I need. The words of Paul to the Christians in Philippi come to mind: "And my God will supply every need of yours according to his riches in glory in Christ Jesus" (Phil. 4:19).

The moon rises full, round, and mellow over the silent wilderness. The campfire burns into a soft bed of glowing embers. The chill of the late hour penetrates my clothing. I seek tranquility in the warm, fluffy down of a sleeping bag. In the darkness I hear the haunting hooting of an owl. Sleep comes.

# Running and Praying
## in Old Town

*We lift our eyes from the city horizon*
*and let them play over the entire*
*hemisphere of the sky....*

— William Beebe

The slightest touch of fall wafts through the morning air. Fall is my favorite season; it is when I feel fresh and vital. I am more alive during this season when death is on the wing than any other time of the year. Fall will not arrive officially, according to my wall calendar for another two weeks. Yet the distant blue of the sky and the receding orange sun tells me I will not have to wait much longer to experience the season's beauty.

Today's seven o'clock hour finds me in the historic district of our friendly village of Pensacola. The crisp bite of the new day and the beauty of my ancient surroundings tell me I must put in a run. These days running requires more effort than it did twenty years ago. The stiffness in my joints whispers there will be no more sub-forty-minute ten kilometer races, no more six-minute miles, no more marathons. At this period in my life I am content to place one foot ahead of the other and cover a mile in ten minutes. My victories come in lathering up a sweat, in working my cardiovascular system, and in losing myself for an hour in dreams and fantasies that never will come true.

The Pensacola historic district is an enchanting part of the city in which to run or walk. The area is filled with stately churches, elegant in their antiquity, with museums and restored hundred-year-old homes transformed into office buildings and restaurants. Even the modern shops and businesses blend into the historical setting with their Spanish and antebellum veneers. The district brings out a feeling of peace from somewhere deep inside of me. As I lean against my truck, going through a routine of stretching exercises, I find myself focused and centered, fused with wonder and reverence. I cannot explain these rumblings that stir around in my hidden depths like a gentle whirlpool; but when I traverse these time honored brick streets, my life slows down and I touch something holy. In spite of the pre-workout stretching routine, my legs feel stiff as I begin this morning's run. My route takes me from the Quayside Art Gallery where I parked, past the Cultural Center into Seville Square. The windblown oak trees and empty benches of Fountain Park come into view on my right. On my left stands the vintage gazebo where orchestras, combos, and quartets make music on Thursday evenings in the summer. Seville Square is a pastoral place. If people spent more time in places like this tranquil spot, there would be less brutality in the world.

Slowly and with effort I plod my way around the quaint square of grass, oak trees, and empty swing sets and jog toward Palafox Street. Palafox is a pleasant strip with its brick sidewalks and galleries. The street was named after a Spanish general who governed Pensacola during the years Spain owned this part of Florida. I run north on Palafox Street past the Saenger Theater, the Iron Gate curio shop, and the Civil War Museum. The red traffic light on Garden Street brings me to a screeching halt, and I sigh a prayer of relief for the chance to catch my breath. The signal flashes to green, and I continue my pilgrimage past the empty building which once housed the Pensacola Little Theater, up the steep hill approaching the Confederate monument, to the intersection with Cervantes Street.

Cervantes Street becomes my turnaround point. I enjoy the downhill run along the opposite side of Palafox. The wind is at my back and my thoughts are saturated with memories. The first time I ran down old Palafox was in May 1981. The run was the Fiesta of Five Flags ten-thousand meter race. I was young and strong and hungry to win a trophy. My finishing time for that race was thirty-eight minutes, nineteen seconds—the swiftest ten kilometers I ever clocked. I zipped through the chute, clicked my stopwatch, and guzzled a free soft drink in the park. Today I run slower and discover a world I could not see twenty years ago.

Bayfront Auditorium barricades the south end of Palafox Street. The rectangular building—home to wrestling matches, craft exhibits, and political rallies—sits on concrete pilings over Pensacola Bay; it is surrounded by water to the east, south, and west. I make my way along the red brick walkway near the auditorium and gaze out across the bottomless blue water. A fleet of fishing vessels is putting out to sea, some of the ships already disappearing into the expansive horizons.

My time piece reads a few minutes past eight o'clock. My morning workout comes to an end. I sit on a bench in Ferdinand Plaza and give thanks for this blessed state of rest. The statue of Andrew Jackson stands to my left; a flowing fountain, to my right. On a nearby bench a bicyclist wearing a green pullover reads the morning newspaper. I feel the chill of a stiffening wind blow against my sweaty shirt. I close my eyes and offer praise to the God who gave me this moment of wonder. I am at peace.

# Seeking Christ
# in the Clouds

*In beauty I move to the direction of*
*the rising sun. In beauty I move to*
*the direction traveling with the sun.*
*In beauty I move to the direction of*
*the setting sun.*

— Navajo Chant

My flight speeds along the runway at seven o'clock, the earliest Delta flight out of our little village this Saturday morning. This is the first time I have flown Delta Airlines; the prospect of flying in a jumbo aircraft is more appealing to me than getting bumped around on one of the smaller commuter flights.

Flying is risky business regardless of whether one is aboard a large jet or a small propeller craft; nevertheless, I like the thought of being aboard a large carrier. At least the bigger airplanes have flight attendants and restrooms to make the trip more comfortable.

I settle into a window seat one row behind the bulkhead separating coach from first class. The English would call coach seating arrangements cozy. I call them just plain cramped. The two seats to my left are occupied. A young lady absorbed in a paperback novel occupies the aisle seat. In the middle seat, next to me, sits a young man in his early thirties with brown hair. I extend my hand and introduce myself; he grunts out the name John before withdrawing into his tortoise shell.

I sense the anxiety building within me as the powerful jet engines roar with increasing intensity and lift the blue and white bird into the sky. Anxiety is a human response when we lose control of our circumstances; at least, that's what I tell myself. "And taking off is less frightening than landing," I muse, attempting to inject a moment of calm into the white-knuckle experience.

The aircraft levels off after a steep climb and bank which lasts several minutes. A carpet of fluffy white hugs our underbelly. Passengers seem to breathe a sigh of relief now that the plane has reached flying altitude. Some unbuckle their seat belts and move toward the restrooms. Others dig out books or laptop computers from their carry-on luggage. Still others lose themselves in the music piped into their heads through earphones. A flight attendant moves with professional poise along the narrow walkway as she serves soft drinks, fruit juice, and coffee.

When the flight attendant reaches the row where I am sitting, I ask for a glass of tomato juice. The attendant opens a can of the thick, red liquid and pours it into a clear plastic cup filled with ice. She wedges a slice of lemon onto the cup's rim and passes it to me. The quiet buzz of conversation blends with the hum of jet engines to form a bubble of silence. I close my eyes and enter the fragile domain of prayer where God awaits. Lord Jesus Christ, Son of God, have mercy on me, a sinner. Lord Jesus Christ, Son of God, have mercy on me, a sinner. This ancient prayer known as the Jesus Prayer offers comfort to my anxious spirit as it did to the Desert Fathers who prayed the same petition almost two thousand years ago. My thoughts come to rest on the various traditions which have contributed to the evangelical Christian faith I embrace. As I reflect on the countless numbers of saints, sinners, and pilgrims who have lived in service to God and died with the expectation that a better life awaited them, I find myself drawn to the simple, unnamed Russian peasant who spent his life walking from village to village, carrying only a Bible and a pinch of salt, praying the Jesus Prayer. Lord Jesus Christ, Son of God, have mercy on me, a sinner.

The older I grow, the more I am haunted by the sins of my youth. The longer I live in a family, the more aware I become of my failures as a husband and father. The longer I serve the Lord Jesus Christ as a pastor and preacher, the more I recognize my inadequacies as a minister of the Gospel. My only hope for receiving forgiveness for my sins is the mercy of the Lord Jesus Christ. The Jesus Prayer takes me beyond rote recitation; it expresses the deepest cry of my heart.

I also find inner strength in praying the Psalms.

"Blessed is the man who walks not in the counsel of the wicked, nor stands in the way of sinners, nor sits in the seat of scoffers; but his delight is in the law of the Lord, and on his law he meditates day and night. He is like a tree planted by streams of water, that yields its fruit in its season, and its leaf does not wither. In all that he does, he prospers" (Ps. 1:1-3). My thoughts shift to those whose lives have become interwoven with my life across the decades—Ella, David, and Matthew. Loving God, I place them in your hands. I wrap them in the blanket of your comforting love. May your will find its expression in their lives. May they become the persons you want them to become. May they experience the abundance of life you desire them to experience.

A gradual left turn nudges me out of my ruminations and draws me back into the reality of flight. My stomach flutters ever so slightly as we begin our descent into Hartsfield International Airport in Atlanta. Out of the sun and into the clouds, we enter the world below. A maze of black asphalt litters a landscape dotted with concrete and steel. In a few moments I will push my way off the airplane and through a churning sea of humanity laden with carry-on luggage. I will scurry down a flight of stairs to catch a robot-run tram that waits for no one, while the voice in my head cries, "Hurry! Hurry! You will miss your connecting flight to Lexington!"

But, right now, the world is still a thousand feet below. So for a few more precious seconds I will sit here and enjoy my quiet time with Christ in the clouds.

# Praying on a Stormy Morning

*The first thing the Lord teaches his
disciples is that they must have a
secret place for prayer; every one
must have some solitary spot where
he can be alone with his God.*

— Andrew Murray

There came a morning when the sun did not shine, when rain tumbled from a blackened sky and landed in puddles on the soaked ground. There came a morning when I stumbled through the darkness to my place of prayer and sought the illumination of the Light of the World.

O Holy Spirit of God, let the radiant light of Jesus Christ illumine my darkened heart and fill my empty soul. Let his purity cleanse me. Let his goodness satisfy me. Let his brilliance guide me.

Allow the radiance of Christ to shine into my eyes

that I may see as Christ sees. Let me look upon the beauty of the world and offer praise. Let me look upon the suffering of the world and be moved to compassion. Let me gaze upon my fellow men and women and see the image of God stamped upon their souls. May I envision people, not as they exist in this broken, fallen world, but as who they can become when touched by grace.

Allow the radiance of Christ to penetrate my mind that I may think as Christ thinks. Give me self-control so that my thoughts may dwell upon the pure rather than the impure, the honorable rather than the dishonorable, and the lovely rather than the unlovely. May my ruminations focus on peace instead of war, on brotherhood instead of discord, and on happiness instead of sorrow. Help me to use my mental faculties to build up rather than to tear down, to encourage rather than to discourage, and to offer hope in the place of despair.

Allow the radiance of Christ to form my words that I may speak as Christ speaks. Let me speak lovingly to those without love. Let me hold out hope to those who have no hope. Let me impart comforting thoughts to those who lack comfort. Let me speak reassuringly to those overwhelmed by fear and anxiety. Let me voice concern for those who have no one to care for them. Let me offer words of cheer to the depressed, challenge to the complacent, and forgiveness to the guilty.

Allow the radiance of Christ to fill my ears that I may hear as Christ hears. Let me know the lyrical note of the songbird, the gentle splash of rain, and the deep silence of the winter snow. Let me discern the gleeful squeals of children at play and the contented sighs of old men at rest.

O Holy Spirit, let not the melody of your world deafen me to the thunderous cries of human misery. Enable me to detect the lonely cry of the aged echoing down the antiseptic corridors of nursing homes. Let me hear the hopeless howl of youth ensnared in the inner cities, victims of poverty, crime, and drugs. Make me sensitive to the desperate sobs of spouses trapped in relationships that died long ago. Help me to comprehend the cry of betrayal from those who have chased status, power, and success; the roar of anger from the powerless victims of injustice; and the whine of remorse from those entangled in sin. Allow the radiance of Christ to touch my hands that I may open them to the needy. May my hands break bread for the hungry, wipe pain from the bleeding forehead, and wash the feet of the dirty. May my hands support the weak, mop the fevered brow, and bring a gentle caress to a harsh world. Strengthen these hands of mine so that they may take up the cross and beckon all to worship the Savior who died on it.

Allow the radiance of Christ to strengthen my feet that I may take the pathways my Savior took. Give me humility that I may walk the path of sacrifice and servanthood, for this is my highest calling. Give me a loving attitude that I may walk the path of compassion and mercy, for when I do it unto the least of these my brethren I do it unto you. Give me courage that I may walk the path of humiliation and betrayal, for it leads me to Calvary. Give me a sense of your presence that I may walk the path of grace, for it brings me to eternal glory.

Allow the radiance of Christ to fill my heart that I may love as Christ loves, hurt as Christ hurts, weep as Christ weeps, empathize as Christ empathizes, and overflow with joy as Christ overflows with joy.

O Holy Spirit of God, in this quiet moment while the world sleeps, I open my empty, lonely self to you. Not one dark corner within the chambers of my heart do I withhold from your radiant brilliance and purifying light. I give myself to you completely so that I may belong to you eternally. Do with me according to your will. Fill me to overflowing or pour me out. Lift me up or break me down. I am yours. My only desire is to do your bidding and to be the person you call me to be. In the holy name of Jesus, let it be so.

# PART 4

# *Hermits*

# Spending Time
# with Thomas Merton

*Your cell will teach you all things.*
— Abba Moses

Thomas Merton has become a trusted companion over
the last ten years. Merton was a Trappist monk who
lived at the Abbey of Gethsemani near Bardstown,
Kentucky. I encountered Merton's writings while
researching a dissertation on the role of silence and
solitude in spiritual formation.

Merton was born in the quaint village of Prades,
France in 1915. His father, Owen Merton, was an
artist from New Zealand. His mother, Ruth Jenkins
Merton, was an artist from the United States. Owen
and Ruth met in Paris where Ruth was studying art

and where Owen was a penniless painter. They married in 1913.

Ruth Merton died when Tom was six years old. Tom Merton spent much of his childhood traveling with his Bohemian artist father. After Owen Merton's death, when Tom was fourteen, his care fell to a guardian who had been a friend of his father. Thomas Merton spent his adolescent years in English boarding schools. He spent holidays and vacations hiking alone across Europe with a rucksack on his back. These solitary excursions, during which young Merton became fascinated with the ruins of ancient churches and monasteries, proved to be a powerful influence on his later spiritual development.

When he was a young man, Thomas Merton enrolled at Cambridge, but was expelled for fathering a child out of wedlock. He came to the United States where his maternal grandparents lived on Long Island and entered Columbia University. Merton received his degree in English literature from Columbia and accepted a faculty position at St. Bonaventure University. He was on the verge of a respectable career in academia when in December 1941 he entered the monastery at Bardstown. Merton took monastic vows and spent the remainder of his life as a monk of Gethsemani, seldom leaving the monastery except to keep medical appointments in nearby Louisville. His final years at Gethsemani were marked by brief trips to California and Alaska. Merton died of accidental electrocution while attending an ecumenical church conference in Bangkok, Thailand;

he stepped from the shower in his motel room and turned on a defective electric fan.

Merton's years at Gethsemani illuminated his conflicting needs to remain hidden from the world while revealing himself to it. Through personal correspondence, articles, and books, Merton expressed his views on subjects ranging from meditation and contemplation to peace activism. His literary works were always set against the background of his growing desire for solitude. Merton confided his need for solitude to his ecclesiastical superiors, who responded that his real need was for "inner solitude, a detachment, a hermitage of the heart." As Merton's spirituality ripened into mature faith, his abbot granted him longer periods of time alone, first in a small tool shed near the monastery and later in a cinder block building on the monastery grounds. Merton called the tiny house his hermitage. Three years before his death he received permission to live there as a hermit.

From a detached academic perspective, I find no argument with the counsel of Merton's ecclesiastical superiors when he requested a place of solitude. Merton's abbot wisely discerned the monk's real requirement was for inner stillness. Solitude of the heart forms the core of the discipline of silence. Until the inner self grows calm, no hidden place of solitude can collect the scattered pieces of our fragmented souls. We can sit alone in the serenity of the chapel or stroll the garden path at sunrise; but without inner serenity the mental voices that demand our attention continue to clamor, and we miss the hushed message that the still, small voice whispers in our ear. When we discover the "hermitage of the heart," as Merton's superiors called it, then geography ceases to matter. When we discover interior silence, we no longer need a lonely mountain or an empty expanse of forest to experience solitude. We can enter the silence even in a room filled with laughing, jabbering people.

A few spiritual masters stumble on the key to the inner sanctuary after a lifetime of searching for it. Their hearts become insulated from the confusion of external circumstances. Their souls find the tranquility they need in order to remain centered on God in the push and shove of the crowd. Their requirement for a time and place in which to be solitary vanishes like the quiet morning mist. But most of us have not mounted the pedestal of spiritual sainthood. Most of us plod our way through our personal worlds of haste and fret one halting step at a time. We are pilgrims of the soul, not masters. We require a physical place of solitude, some secluded spot where we can become reacquainted with ourselves and reconnect with God.

As I reflect on my fast-paced existence during these productive years, like Thomas Merton I discover an urgency to maintain a respectful distance from individuals and society. Solitude helps me to maintain my sanity when everyone around me seems insane and when my daily schedule spins out of control. It is not enough for me to be inwardly solitary, detached from my surroundings while still in them. I must experience actual solitude. I must enter those moments and places where no one else goes. Sometimes, I liken my search for solitude during these busy years to that of a Bedouin searching for an oasis. I have become a spiritual nomad making my way across an endless desert of activity in search of peace and quiet. The friction created by my active vocation blisters my soul. The blowing desert sand dries up the wells of living water that once flowed within me. My spirit withers under the relentless heat of chronic busyness. Sometimes I stumble upon a momentary oasis of silence and solitude. When I do, I pause along the journey to drink from the oasis's crystal pools. I cool myself beneath the breeze of swaying palms and suck the sweet nectar of the succulent dates. Refreshed, I continue on my way. The journey is not easy; but it is worth the effort.

# Pondering the Benefits of a Cocoon

*Serious things have to be done in silence. In silence men love, pray, listen, compose, paint, write, think, and suffer. This is the ministry of solitude.*

— Ralph Harper

Cocooning! University of Chicago church historian Martin Marty uses the term cocooning to describe a growing social trend in America.

Marty's observations of the lifestyles and behavior patterns of technological humanity lead him to conclude that many Americans are terrified of the culture in which they live. Many are afraid of AIDS; they fear people who have AIDS, and they fear contracting the disease themselves. People fear that the crime in the streets will invade their homes. They fear the prospect of losing their jobs through corporate down-sizing. They fear big government. They fear their children will fall victim to the excesses of the drug and pleasure culture which surrounds them.

Marty notes that, in response to their phobias, a growing number of individuals drop out of society. They withdraw from the mainstream of public life every chance they get. They spend as much time as possible holed up in comfortable hideaways like beachfront condominiums and lakeside cabins. They retreat into their cocoons and remain dormant as long as they can, until their jobs or other responsibilities require them to emerge.

Marty observes that, while cocooning may be one of several forms of antisocial behavior common to modern America, the phenomenon has a strong appeal to an overworked, highly stressed populace. Marty interviewed self-confessed caterpillars; all said they feel safe wrapped in their cocoons and enjoy the time they spend in them. The caterpillars agreed that cocooning affords them the opportunity to pursue hobbies and activities they cannot pursue when engaged in their work or involved in relationships. Cocooning provides all of us with the time and space we need to be alone, away from people and chores. Cocooning allows us to put distance between ourselves and our occupations, bosses and time clocks.

It lets us momentarily walk away from the demands of children, parents, and spouses. In the solitude of the cocoon we experience the freedom to engage in activities that nurture us and bring us pleasure. We can read, write, or paint; ride a bicycle, walk, or jog. We can pray, meditate, and reflect; sleep, snack, or watch television. In the cocoon we can give ourselves to those pursuits that nourish our souls and renew our weary spirits without having to answer to anyone for the way we spend our time.

The growing popularity of cocooning presents us with a dilemma. The trend forces us to ask, "Where does our duty lie?" Does our primary responsibility lie in making a contribution to society; in using our talents, resources, energies, and intellects to improve the community we fear and seek to avoid? Or is our foremost duty to ourselves, to care for personal needs and enrich our lives?

The dilemma between serving society or being true to ourselves is not unique to modern America. The Greek philosopher Socrates confronted the same issue in Athens in the fifth century B.C. In ancient Greece a citizen's duty to the city-state was considered to be of paramount importance. Contributing to society was understood to be the highest attainment any citizen could achieve, until Socrates began teaching the significance of the quest for personal truth. The emphasis Socrates placed on individuality and his disdain for public opinion led not to the resolution of the debate, but to the philosopher's imprisonment and execution. Every student of philosophy knows the story of Socrates calmly downing the cup of poison hemlock.

The divergent schools of thought which created conflict in ancient Athenian society continue to create controversy in twenty-first century America. Contemporary Socratic philosophers argue that the needs of the individual remain more important than service to society. Consequently, antisocial patterns such as cocooning easily find justification. Activists contend that contributing to the welfare of the community is of supreme importance. As a result, men and women run for public office, teach school, go into ministry, and become physicians, missionaries, and social workers.

After three decades of living the public life of a pastor and making a contribution to society, I find myself choosing to retreat into my cocoon and lie dormant for awhile. I would like to think my proclivity for cocooning is not a reaction against a busy, public life. I prefer to believe my desire to live in a cocoon is a necessary part of my active life, the aspect of my existence which renews me and allows me to make additional contributions to the community.

Georg W. F. Hegel, the influential German philosopher, might express my understanding of cocooning in terms of thesis, antithesis and synthesis. Cocooning is not the antithesis, the opposite, of societal involvement. Cocooning is the synthesis, the resolution, which grows out of the conflict between complete immersion in society and permanent withdrawal from society .

I regret that Socrates and Hegel lived in different centuries, and could not sit down across the table from one another and have a good heart-to-heart talk. The two philosophers might have discovered they had a lot in common. A little probing of one another's thoughts, a few hours of philosophical give-and-take might have made the cup of hemlock unnecessary.

Here's to one form of antisocial behavior.

# Considering the Eremitical Lifestyle

*What the solitary renounces is not his union with other men, but rather the deceptive fictions...which tend to take the place of genuine social unity.*

— James Finley

An eremite is a religious hermit, an individual who chooses to live apart from society in order to experience more completely his religious faith. The eremite often makes his home in lonely places off the beaten path surrounded by wilderness. His companions are the squirrels scurrying from tree limb to tree limb and the songbirds opening their throats to herald the freshness of the new day. The eremite listens to the wind whistling through the forest; he hears the rumble of rolling thunder as it drifts across the sky. These simple movements of nature give wings to the eremite's heart and call to his mind the God he seeks.

When a person decides to live the eremitical lifestyle, he not only chooses to live exclusively for God; he rejects the standards and values of the world which he leaves behind. He turns his back on everything the world considers important. He walks away from the quest for material possessions, the pursuit of status, and the unbridled passion of ambition. He declares a resounding "no" to the need for societal approval and the temptation to self-aggrandizement. For the eremite, no way of life other than solitude is possible. To live in community and embrace community mores means death for him—the slow, agonizing, excruciating death of the soul. Society frequently rejects the religious hermit for a number of reasons. Society rejects him because it does not understand him. Men and women who live in community often have difficulty comprehending why one would choose to live alone for God.

Society rejects the eremite because the eremite makes society uncomfortable. In choosing the life of the religious hermit, the eremite exposes the superficial values which persons who spend their lives in community tend to cherish. His courage in living alone exposes the cowardice of the herd mentality. His simplicity in surviving on the barest essentials, without modern conveniences, exposes society's complexity. His sacrificial mode of existence condemns society's greed. His hunger to know God accuses society's appetite for false deities. Those accustomed to living in community often find the prospect of isolation terrifying. They fear the thought of living apart, of living by themselves.

## Society's Need for the Eremite

The relationship between the eremite and society is paradoxical. Society embraces the religious hermit at the same time that it shuns him. Society draws the hermit into its heart with the same arms with which it pushes him away.

The eremite accepts the severe conditions of his solitary existence. He cherishes his solitude. In solitude he finds the nurture, renewal, and rebirth his soul requires. The eremite is most alive when he is most alone. The silence becomes his bread; the stillness, his drink; and the tranquility, his life blood. He smiles with patient understanding at the fears society harbors for his austere lifestyle. Confronting himself in solitude does not intimidate the eremite. Many persons who live in community recognize the eremite's courage; they respect his decision to live alone and dedicate himself to God.

Since the eremite earns the respect of segments of society, some men and women who live in community seek the eremite for spiritual guidance. In the

Russian tradition of spiritual formation, the poustinik is a religious hermit who shares the wisdom he gains through his solitary existence with those who come to him.

The poustinik begins his spiritual pilgrimage unaware of the journey on which he is about to embark. He is an ordinary peasant living in his village and going about the chores of village life. He knows his neighbors and is known by them. His years pass in the obscurity of everyday life.

When the obscure village peasant hears the whisper of God in his ear, when he feels the gentle touch of the divine hand on his shoulder, and when in response he disappears into the vast Russian forest to enter his poustinia and embrace the eremitical life of prayer and physical labor, his former villagers begin tracking a path to his door. The neighbors who once casually spoke to him on the village lane now make pilgrimages to the poustinik's humble cabin, seeking a word from God the holy man offers.

Henry David Thoreau is another example of the hermit besieged by society. The nineteenth century transcendentalist, naturalist, and writer feared he would come to the end of his years only to discover he had not lived. In an attempt to experience the full measure of life, Thoreau withdrew from his community of Concord, Massachusetts and lived alone for two years in a small cabin on the banks of Walden Pond. Thoreau expressed his love for solitude in a letter to a friend: "O solitude, obscurity. . . .

I never triumph so as when I have the least success in my neighbor's eyes."

In spite of Thoreau's determination to live a hermit's existence, the naturalist never lacked for companionship in his unpretentious home by Walden Pond. In his account of life in the woods, Thoreau recounts how neighbors from Concord and nearby farms frequently paid him visits and spent afternoons talking and sitting on the porch of his cabin.

Thoreau's acquaintances called on him during his two years at Walden Pond for the same reasons the Russian villagers seek out the poustinik. The eremite possesses an intangible quality which attracts those of us who live in community. We admire the eremite's courage in living the solitary existence devoted to God. We sense that the hermit's lifestyle provides him with spiritual depth and wisdom not experienced by those of us who live in society. We believe that the religious hermit, in feeding his soul on the bread of life and drinking from the well of living water, can satisfy our spiritual appetites and quench our souls' thirsts.

## Final Thoughts on the Eremitical Lifestyle

The world fears and respects the eremite. Society rejects him yet embraces him. The eremite is both renegade and hero to those of us who live in community. He reminds us of the deceptions under which many of us live; at the same time he calls us to a more authentic existence. As a lighthouse stands on the rocky shoreline signaling ships against the perils of the coastal shoals, the eremite stands on the edge of society warning against the dangers of shallow living and lighting the way into the deeper life of the Spirit.

# Ruminating on
# Father Arsenius

*Settle yourself in solitude and you*
*will come upon Him in yourself.*
— St. Teresa of Avila

In *The Way of the Heart*, Henri Nouwen relates the story of Father Arsenius, one of the more well-known Desert Fathers. Father Arsenius was an educated, respected Roman citizen with considerable political power in ancient Rome. Arsenius lived at the palace of Emperor Theodosius where he served as tutor to the princes Arcadius and Honorius. Father Arsenius was a man of religious conviction as well as arts and letters. He often prayed, "Lord, lead me in the way of salvation."

One day as Arsenius was asking God to guide him along the path of salvation, he heard a voice saying to him, "Arsenius, flee the world and you will be saved." In response to the divine command, Arsenius left Rome and sailed to Alexandria, Egypt. In Alexandria, Father Arsenius continued to beseech God to bring him to salvation. Again he heard the heavenly voice. This time God declared, "Flee, be silent and pray always, for these are the sources of sinlessness."

Eventually Father Arsenius, in obedience to God's command, left the world of art, education, and civilization he had known. He withdrew into the desert where he spent the remainder of his life in prayer and physical labor.

The aspect of Father Arsenius's personality which inspires me most is his courage. Father Arsenius found the courage to listen to the divine voice and respond obediently when the voice called him into the desert. Courage to respond to grace seems to be the element that separates true disciples of Christ from the would-be disciples. The Gospel of Mark recounts how Peter, Andrew, James, and John left their fishing to follow Jesus when invited to do so.

"And passing along by the Sea of Galilee, he saw Simon and Andrew the brother of Simon casting a net in the sea; for they were fishermen. And Jesus said to them, 'Follow me and I will make you become fishers of men.'" And immediately they left their nets and followed him (Mk. 1:16-18). "And going on a little farther, he saw James the son of Zebedee and John his brother, who were in their boat mending the nets. And immediately he called them; and they left their father Zebedee in the boat with the hired servants, and followed him" (Mk. 1:19-20). Mark tells us that the calling of Levi, the tax collector, came in much the same way as the calling of the four Galilean fishermen. "And as he passed on, he saw Levi the son of Alphaeus sitting at the tax office, and he said to him, 'Follow me.' And he rose and followed him" (Mk. 2:14). The immediate, unhesitating response of Peter, Andrew, James, John, and Levi when Jesus summoned them to discipleship stands in sharp contrast to the response of the Rich Young Ruler. The Rich Young Ruler came to Jesus seeking the way to eternal life. He affirmed that he had observed the commandments of the law from childhood. Perceiving the young man's attachment to material possessions, Jesus instructed him to give everything he owned to the poor. "Then come, follow me," Jesus advised. When the wealthy young man heard the demand which discipleship placed on him, he turned and walked away.

Jesus called the Rich Young Ruler to discipleship with the same words he used to call his five faithful apostles. "Follow me," the Lord declared to each of them. But the Rich Young Ruler did not obey the divine command. He lacked the courage to give up that aspect of his life which was most important to him, his wealth.

The Gospel of Luke recounts the tragic story of two unnamed people who wanted to become followers of Jesus, but who were unwilling to make the sacrifices discipleship required them to make. The first would-be disciple told Jesus, "I will follow you wherever you go" (Luke 9:57). Jesus warned that discipleship might require the man to give up his home and comfortable lifestyle. "Foxes have holes, and birds of the air have nests; but the Son of man has nowhere to lay his head," the Lord declared (Luke 9:58). This would-be follower of Jesus confronted the same stumbling block the Rich Young Ruler faced. He discovered that discipleship is more than a mere flirtation with the Gospel; discipleship involves a complete commitment of every aspect of one's life to Christ. The second would-be disciple said to Jesus, "I will follow you, Lord; but let me first say farewell to those at my home" (Luke 9:61). This man placed conditions on his service which Jesus was unwilling to accept. In response to his offer, Jesus cautioned, "No one who puts his hand to the plow and looks back is fit for the kingdom of God" (Luke 9:62).

To the companion of the two would-be disciples, Jesus issued the familiar invitation, "Follow me" (Luke 9:59). Yet this person, like his friends, proved unwilling to surrender to the demands of discipleship. He told Jesus he wanted to bury his father before he would be willing to assume the responsibilities following Christ involved. Jesus replied, "Leave the dead to bury their own dead; but as for you, go and proclaim the kingdom of God" (Luke 9:60).

The call to Christian discipleship is a universal

one; Jesus invites all of us to follow him. Each individual's call takes a unique form in accordance with God's plan for his or her life. Some of us, like Father Arsenius, hear the divine voice compelling us to flee the world and live in solitude. Others like Peter, Andrew, James, John and Levi receive the divine commission to proclaim the Good News of Jesus Christ to a world which desperately needs to hear good news. The issue each of us must face when we hear and understand God's call is, "Do I have the courage to say 'yes' to God?"

There was a period in my life many years ago when I felt confident about the nature of God's call to me. I understood that God had commissioned me to preach the Gospel. Thirty years later, as I find myself attracted to the contemplative lifestyle, I no longer feel as certain about the nature of my divine call. Toward the end of his life, Henri Nouwen questioned whether being faithful to his calling meant that his vocation must remain the same as it had been for many years. I find myself wrestling with the same question.

However the issue works itself out in my life, I make only one request of God. I ask for the courage to obey the divine voice. I do not want to deny the Christ who loves me and saves me. Like Father Arsenius, I want to be a faithful disciple of Jesus, whatever discipleship means.

# Probing the Thoughts
## of Peter France

*Society is dominated by the inane*
*notion that action is the only reality.*
— Richard J. Foster

Peter France resides in Devon, England but he spends much of his time living the semi-eremitical lifestyle on the island of Patmos. For the last two thousand years, Patmos has been the home of both secular and religious hermits.

Patmos is one of a group of Greek islands known as the Sporades in the Aegean Sea. The island is ten miles long by five miles wide. Most of its terrain is volcanic rock. In biblical times the Roman Empire banished political prisoners to Patmos. Patmos was the island to which the apostle John was exiled around

94 A.D. because of his faith in Jesus Christ. It was during this time that John experienced his vision of the risen Christ and penned the book of Revelation.

Today the island of Patmos continues to provide a home for individuals who do not fit the mold of society. The recluses who live there make their abodes in dilapidated houses, lean-tos, and caves hidden among the island's remote volcanic valleys.

In 1996 Peter France wrote an insightful volume about persons who sought the reclusive lifestyle. *Hermits: The Insights of Solitude* traces the development of the solitary life from its early stages in China to modern hermits like Robert Lax, a colleague of Thomas Merton, who now lives a hermit life on Patmos. France notes the focus on individualism as an avenue to personal fulfillment appeared in China in the sixth century B.C. in the teachings of Lao-Tse. While Confucius contended discharging one's obligations to society was the way to happiness and serenity, Lao-Tse argued that avoiding social responsibility was the path to contentment.

France's section on ornamental hermits proves enthralling. The chapter deals with the attitude of many Europeans toward hermits from the mid to late eighteenth century. Much of Europe came under the influence of two contrasting schools of thought then, those of Diderot and Rousseau. Diderot argued that humanity was created to enjoy society; Rousseau espoused contemplation on the beauty of nature. European society was so torn between these opposing philosophies that some of the landed aristocracy, out of their sensitivity to political correctness, opted to embrace both the social and the reclusive lifestyles at the same time. France relates the account of an English gentleman Hamilton who sought to discharge his obligations to both philosophies by hiring a hermit to live on his estate in Surrey while Hamilton led the existence of a social butterfly.

That conflicting approach reflects the ambivalence many cultures feel toward those who reject societal norms in favor of the hermit's life. America places a high premium on usefulness. We are a utilitarian culture. We recognize as worthwhile those persons who are industrious, who live useful lives, and who serve functional purposes. If a person opts for the contemplative, retiring existence, we often label that individual of no use, of little value to society. In this sense, America has not evolved far from sixth century China when Confucius argued that humanity found greatest fulfillment in discharging its social obligations.

The conflict I experience between discharging my duty to my fellow men and women and giving priority to personal needs becomes obvious in the choices I make during the course of a day's work. I must decide each day how to use my unstructured time, those hours which are not penciled in with church meetings, counseling sessions, pastoral visitation, Bible study, and sermon preparation. Do I take on tasks that do not require my immediate attention? Must I always be doing something in order to be of value? Or may I spend my free time in activities which my retiring personality finds more to its liking, such as reading, writing and reflecting?

During the years I jogged long distances, I read a satirical article in a runner's magazine. The author, a burned-out marathon runner, was exploring the prospect of hiring someone to run his daily miles for him. The author humorously suggested that his replacement could dress in the author's running shorts and shirt; he could run the routes the author frequently ran, while the author napped on the sofa. The article suggested in tongue-in-cheek fashion that bystanders who observed the replacement runner would not detect the difference between him and the authentic runner.

Perhaps I should consider the merits of hiring a replacement pastor. I could employ an individual who looks, acts, talks and thinks like me; the process would be fairly simple given today's scientific breakthroughs in cloning. I could loan my look-alike my car for conducting pastoral visitation, my Bible commentaries for researching sermons, and my vestments for Sunday services. While he performed all the chores I find so exhausting, I could hike a trail or hang out on the beach. Most of my parishioners would not recognize the difference between the imitation and the authentic pastor. If the eighteenth century Europeans could hire hermits to fulfill their reclusive obligations for them while they enjoyed the pleasures of society, I can hire an extrovert to live the public lifestyle for me while I enjoy the benefits of solitude.

Lao-Tse had the right idea.

# Entering the
# Monastic Silence

*The soul craves experiences that offer*
*it the rich depths of God. Silence,*
*solitude, holy leisure, simplicity,*
*prayer.... All these feed the soul....*

— Sue Monk Kidd

When the church Administrative Council gave me a month sabbatical at the beginning of my eighth year as the church's pastor, I immediately knew what I wanted to do with a portion of that leave. I wanted to spend a few days in silent retreat at a Trappist monastery. In 1974, while a student at Asbury Theological Seminary, I spent a weekend in a Trappist monastery, the Abbey of Gethsemani, near Bardstown, Kentucky. Two fellow seminarians and I made the one-hour drive to the cloister so they could find a quiet place to complete their term papers. I had no term paper to write, but went along at their invitation.

The visit to Gethsemani proved to be the longest forty-eight hours I had spent up to that point in my young life. I had not cultivated an appreciation for silence during those early years. I had not learned how to fill the empty hours with meaningful solitude. Prayer and meditation were not part of my vocabulary nor my experience. While my companions were engrossed in footnotes and annotated bibliographies, I walked the cavernous halls of Gethsemani, twiddling my thumbs and listening to the loud sighs of boredom that escaped from my lips and echoed off the empty walls.

Our brief visit to Gethsemani came during the dead of a harsh Kentucky winter. A three-inch layer of snow covered the monastery's open courtyards and rolling fields like a white blanket. The heat was turned off at night in the retreat house where we stayed. I went home with a painful sore throat.

In the years since that inauspicious introduction to the monastic life, I have grown in my appreciation of these reclusive houses of prayer. My attraction to monasteries has increased in proportion to my desire for silence, solitude, prayer, and meditation. So for a week during my sabbatical, I choose to live apart from the world of rush and worry I experience on a daily basis. I seek the quiet, comfort and seclusion of the Monastery of the Holy Spirit near Conyers, Georgia, a few miles east of the sprawling, surging metropolis of Atlanta.

The Trappist order originated in the village of La Trappe, France in 1664, when a Cistercian monk, Armand de Rance, sought to institute reforms within his monastery. The Trappists came to the United States in the late eighteenth and early nineteenth centuries to escape anti-monastic legislation in France. The Monastery of the Holy Spirit, was founded in 1944, when twenty monks were sent from the Abbey of Gethsemani in Kentucky to establish a monastic presence in Georgia.

The monks of Conyers rise every morning at four o'clock for a period of silent prayer called Vigils. They observe three additional times of daily communal prayer. Morning prayers, called Lauds, are held at seven o'clock. Evening prayers, called Vespers, are held at five-thirty; and Compline, a period of prayer before bedtime, is observed at eight-fifteen. In between these times of prayer, the monks live a simple lifestyle revolving around spiritual reading and physical labor.

## The First Day of Silence

My brief venture into monastic silence begins this August evening with the six o'clock supper hour. There are approximately twenty-five retreatants in the forty-seat dining room. The meal of tuna salad, egg salad, carrot salad, and wheat bread is eaten in silence. Silence is observed throughout the retreat house just as it is in the cloisters where the monks reside. At first the silence feels awkward to me; but it does not take long for me to get comfortable with the lack of interaction among the strangers sitting at the table. The silence of the dining room stands in bold contrast to the television chatter that usually fills my house during mealtime.

Following the evening meal, I settle into my room in the retreat house and attend Compline in the cathedral. I sit in the shadows in the back of the church and observe the monks and oblates moving with peaceful rhythm through the chants, prayers, and readings which signal the end of their day. The lights are on only over the chancel. The soft glow at the front of the church creates an atmosphere of holiness and serenity. As the incense wafts through the rafters toward heaven, I reflect on the words of John in the Revelation: "and the smoke of the incense rose with the prayers of the saints" (Rev. 8:4).

Compline lasts thirty minutes. I sit quietly in my pew, unsure of when to stand and when to bow throughout the unfamiliar ritual. I reflect on the fact that Jesus Christ came into the world to tear down the walls that separate us from each other. The apostle Paul expressed it beautifully in his letter to the church in Ephesus: "For he...has broken down the dividing wall. So then you are no longer strangers . . . but you are fellow citizens with the saints and members of the household of God" (Eph. 2:14, 19). When God looks on creation, God does not see us as Roman Catholics or Baptists or Methodists, evangelicals or liberals, clergy or laity. God sees us as beloved children, those for whom Jesus Christ died on the cross to save from sin. God understands our struggles and fears which divide us. God offers us unmerited love and abundant mercy.

Sleep comes easily following Compline as the monastery enters the great silence of the night.

## The Second Day of Silence

Today is the second day of my retreat into silence and solitude at the Monastery of the Holy Spirit. I arrived yesterday, the noise of uncertainty clamoring within. The inner rush was so complete that my pulse raced and my breath came in gasps. But the tranquility which pervades this monastery is compelling; I find myself drawn into it. As this second day begins, I discover that the palpitations have ceased and my soul waits peacefully before God.

I spend much of this day reading and reflecting on the works of Henri Nouwen. Nouwen was the Dutch priest who, despite his career in academia, found his greatest satisfaction serving as a pastor to the mentally and physically challenged residents of l'Arche Daybreak community in Toronto, Canada. Nouwen touched the lives of thousands through his faculty positions at Notre Dame, Yale, and Harvard, and through his work with the poor in Central and South America. In spite of his untimely death in 1996, his writings continue to minister to millions of readers.

Nouwen's works speak quietly but poignantly to my heart as I immerse myself in the tranquility of this retreat house. I find myself drawn to three of his later books: *Out of Solitude, Can You Drink the Cup?* and *The Genesee Diary.*

In the short but powerful volume *Out of Solitude,* Nouwen explores the relationship between solitude, caring, and living in expectancy, within the context of Christian ministry. Nouwen contends that Christ calls us to enter into the woundedness of the world and do what we can to bring about healing. Before we can become Christ's curative agents, we must cultivate compassion for those who are hurting. Nouwen declares that, when we attempt to cure people without caring about them, we contribute to a greater sense of pain in the people we are trying to help. Nouwen believes solitude helps us become compassionate. In silence and solitude we are nurtured by God and equipped with the empathy that enables us to care about people. Henri Nouwen's insights provide me with a fresh perspective on my pastoral ministry. When I entered the ministry thirty years ago, I felt hopeful and expectant. I felt the unmistakable call of God on my life. I discovered God had given me the gifts of preaching and relating to people in a caring way. No one was more surprised than I to watch these spiritual gifts develop in the years that followed my ordination. I believed my efforts would make a difference in the lives of the people I served. I assumed the initial enthusiasm I felt for pastoral ministry would never diminish.

My career did not turn out the way I anticipated. In spite of my best efforts, in spite of early mornings of prayer and tiring afternoons of caring for the persons in my church, my attempts to make a significant impact on people's spiritual lives produced few results. Somewhere along the line, the excitement of being a pastor gave way to the dull routine of writing sermons and saying perfunctory prayers with patients lying in hospital beds.

Here, in the silence of this monastery, I examine my life as a pastor and confront some unnerving questions. Is the anguish of being a pastor speaking louder these days than the voice of God? Do I remain in parish ministry because my skills lend themselves to local church ministry and allow me to do little other than church work? Do I continue only because it provides me with an income and a roof over my family's head? How long can I continue in a vocation which rewards me with little immediate success?

Even after thirty years, numerous aspects of parish ministry remain foreign to my introverted personality. I am weary of running a church (a term tossed around in ministerial banter as if the church functioned like a corporation and its pastor was the chief executive officer). I am exhausted from making small talk at church suppers and planning revivals where no one comes to the altar to accept Jesus Christ as Lord and Savior. I am tired of the endless routine of attending meetings, raising church budgets, and spending hours writing reports which no one reads. When I took my first church nearly three decades ago, I did not understand that my energies would be consumed by routine responsibilities.

Nouwen's reflections in *Out of Solitude* give me the fresh perspective I need on pastoral ministry, the perspective I saw that Sunday morning when I stepped into the pulpit for the first time. The desires that reverberated through my wildly beating heart that Sunday morning were simply to proclaim the Good News of Jesus Christ, to bring comfort to people who were hurting, and to offer hope to those who felt hopeless. Nouwen reminds me that, ultimately, Christian ministry must be measured not by how much money we raise, nor how large a congregation we serve, nor how skillfully we play the game of church politics, but by how available we make ourselves to people who are struggling to bring order into their chaotic lives.

In the solitude of this monastery, I hear again the call of God and I remember who I am. I am a pastor, and I am grateful to God for the grace which called me into pastoral ministry.

## The Third Day of Silence

Yesterday around five o'clock in the afternoon, following an extended period of reading, reflecting, and writing, I entered a time of meditation as deep and serene as any I have experienced. It was not a state of mind I conjured up and during which I forced myself to remain silent; it was a mode of being into which I slipped naturally following a day of non-speaking. I remained in this meditative trance for thirty minutes, during which time my body relaxed, my breathing fell into a peaceful rhythm, and my thoughts came to rest exclusively on Jesus Christ. The depth and intensity of this meditative state was different from any experienced before, where distractions invade my consciousness and I wonder how long until the alarm on my wristwatch signals the end of the silence. This time, meditation was deep, peaceful, and sweet; it flowed easily. I could have stayed in it longer than thirty minutes had I chosen. The ringing of the vesper bell reminded me I wanted to attend evening prayer.

This period of silent meditation toward the end of the second day seemed to be a transition point in my brief stay at the Holy Spirit Monastery, a moment when the outer world disappeared from consciousness and inner peace began to have its way. The tranquility was so overwhelming that verbal communication seemed inappropriate, even profane. The conversations into which I was drawn afterwards felt unnatural to me, alien to my spirit.

One retreatant approached me as I was walking through the parking lot to the lake. She told me the monastery wells were running low on water. She asked me to contribute toward the purchase of bottled water and disposable plates for the kitchen. Our verbal exchange was important, given the severe summer drought; but the dialogue took my thoughts off God and focused them on other people's problems.

On the third morning of retreat, between Lauds and breakfast, I was sitting in the prayer room reading *The Genesee Diary*, when my suite mate sat down next to me. Mike came to the monastery last night and quickly discovered he did not know what to do with silence and solitude. He spoke of his need to be on retreat, to be away from a stressful job; but he confessed he did not know how to handle the empty time he had encountered since his arrival.

I could not enter into meditation with a clear conscience knowing a fellow retreatant was struggling with his silence. I suggested Mike visit the monastery library or bookstore and select some reading material. I asked Mike if he was familiar with Thomas Merton, the monk of Gethsemani. When Mike indicated he had not heard of Merton, I gave him a quick sketch of the monk's life and suggested he look at Merton's *Thoughts in Solitude*. We discussed Mike's budding desire to write a journal about his spiritual pilgrimage. In spite of my desire for silence, I could not walk away from this young man whose last name I did not know. I understood the uncomfortable sensation of being at loose ends, of not knowing how to fill the emptiness and transform the loneliness into meaningful solitude. Yet, as with the earlier encounter in the monastery parking lot, I came away from this conversation with the feeling that the holy silence had been breached.

As a consequence of the two encounters in which

I felt drawn away from contemplation, I choose to spend the majority of my third day at the monastery in my room. Abba Moses, one of the Desert Fathers, said, "Your cell will teach you all things." Today in my cell I write in my journal; I spend time in prayer, meditation, and reflection; I learn the discipline of being totally alone and of encountering God in the aloneness. How easily spirituality ripens here in my cell, in this environment of monastic silence. The agendas that occupy my attention throughout most days—people, problems, television, food—fall away and become inconsequential. Substantive issues, matters with eternal significance—silence, solitude, prayer, attentive listening to God—become the focus of these moments and days. My heart is quiet and my soul is at peace.

## The Fourth Day of Silence

During my stay at Holy Spirit Monastery, I attend all four of the daily communal prayer offices: Vigils, Lauds, Vespers, and Compline. Vigils is the time of silent meditation before daybreak; the silence of Vigils is broken only by the chanting of the choir monks and the reading of Holy Scripture. The purpose of Vigils is to give thanks for God's protection during the night and to insure that the first utterance the monks make on rising from sleep is a declaration of praise to God.

When I arrived at the monastery, I assumed I would find Vigils to be the most meaningful of the four prayer services. I am a morning person. I enjoy getting up before sunrise and beginning the day with a time of silent reflection. I feel the most creative and do my best work during the morning hours. As the clock winds toward noon, my creative energies begin to run down. Afternoons are usually reserved for work that requires a minimum of concentration. Most days I gradually degenerate into a state of lethargy in which, as evening approaches, I do little except doze in my reclining chair or vegetate in front of some mindless television program. There are nights when I cannot recall falling into bed because I am so exhausted.

To my astonishment I find Compline, not Vigils, to be the most meaningful daily prayer office at Holy Spirit Monastery. The word *compline* means to complete the day; and that is what the service of prayers, chants, readings, and silence does for those who attend. At the end of the service, the monks and retreatants silently exit the shadowy cathedral to enter the great silence, that period between nine o'clock in the evening and four o'clock in the morning when total silence is observed throughout the monastery. The silence is so heavy and the solitude so pervasive that the monks are not permitted to turn on the showers.

Compline touches me profoundly, at a deep level of my being, because I usually neglect to pray at the end of the day. I feel too tired, too scattered, too distracted to enter into God's presence in the evening. I do not have the energy or the focus needed to pray at night. The service of Compline at Holy Spirit Monastery lifts me beyond my usual nightly state of lethargy. Compline gives me a sense of focus almost as intense as the concentration I possess at the beginning of each day. It enables me to think about God, love God, and adore God like I seldom do at that evening hour.

I often enjoy the heavenly Father's voice in the song of the dawn bird. How delightful to sit in the morning silence while the world sleeps, then to hear a single bird awaken and break the stillness with the melody of song. Here at Holy Spirit Monastery I discover the joy of hearing God's voice in the chirp of crickets at twilight.

In the monastery the day begins with God and ends with God. One feels God's quiet but powerful presence throughout the day. I must carry this holiness in my heart when I return to the world.

## Reflections on Leaving the Monastery

I conclude my venture into monastic silence two days ahead of schedule. The monks are closing the retreat house and asking the retreatants to vacate because of a severe water shortage. Holy Spirit Monastery has three deep wells; but the water table has dropped so low due to prolonged drought that all of the wells have gone dry. A ten thousand-gallon supply of water remains; but the monastery requires thirteen thousand gallons per day to operate.

My heart hangs heavy with sorrow at leaving the

silence this holy place offers. I yearn to stay for a few more days. Obedience to the rule is one of the fundamental principles of monastic life. Through obedience to their order and ecclesiatical superiors, monks learn to surrender themselves to God. So when the retreat master asks me to leave before my scheduled departure date, I arrange my belongings in my backpack and make my exit.

As I reflect on my four days there, I am struck by the simplicity of the place. My room was small, but adequate. The furnishings included a bed and bedside table, a desk and chair, and a second chair for reading. There was one lamp on the desk and another beside the bed. The monks call the tiny room a cell; it is the place of spiritual formation.

The meals the retreatants ate were as basic as the rooms where we slept. We ate cold cereal, juice, and fruit for breakfast, and salads and vegetables for lunch and supper. Trappist monks do not eat meat except on special occasions or when they are sick.

The evening meal was called supper rather than dinner, indicating the intimate fellowship that occurs during the meal. The word supper comes from the ancient word sup, meaning to eat slowly and thus make time for fellowship around the table. In a culture of fast-food restaurants, where people gobble down their food on the run and families no longer sit at the table together, we need more places like the Monastery of the Holy Spirit where time and space are created for supper.

The daily routine of the monastic community

centered around a simple life of prayer and work. Prayer periods were private and communal. The work consisted of physical labor. St. Benedict, father of monasticism, believed the balance between the spiritual and the physical helped the monk become aware of God at all times. In a culture of frantic, sometimes mindless activity, where few people scratch the surface of prayer and where work often consists of endless hours of tedious routine, we would do well to adopt the simple lifestyle of our cloistered brothers.

The simplicity of Holy Spirit Monastery was beneficial for me. The silence cleared my head of the noise that afflicts so many of my days. The solitude gave me the space I needed to look into the recesses of my heart; and in doing so, to gain a fresh perspective on where my life has been and where it is going. The periods of private and communal prayer enabled me to adore God who, given the hurried pace of my existence, had become more of a stranger than an intimate companion. I discovered I am usually so busy serving God that I neglect to make time to love God.

During one of the communal prayer services, a monk spoke about how the servants of God in the Bible felt the presence of God surrounding them at all times. The customary term for expressing the presence of God in the Old Testament is *Shekinah*. Shekinah refers to the visible radiance of God's presence that dwelt among God's people. Shekinah is the blessing all quiet moments and holy places bestow upon us; they bring us face-to-face, heart-to-heart with our loving heavenly Father and enable us to experience God's glory.

# About the Author

The Rev. James A. Belcher is an ordained Elder in the United Methodist Church. He has served churches in Alabama and Florida since 1972.

His other works include *Chasing Dinosaurs: Poetic Reflections from Midlife*, and pieces in *The Circuit Rider, The Upper Room*, and *Seek*.